A Canadian Shame - The Indian Act and Residential Schools

A Canadian Shame - The Indian Act and Residential Schools

Darren Grimes

CONTENTS

DEDICATION vii

1 Foreword 1
2 Preface 11
3 Definitions 15
4 Notable Players 19
   Timelines 27
5 Timeline of The Indian Act 29
6 Residential Schools 33
7 The International Tribunal for the Disappeared 47
   The Ugly 63
8 Tuberculosis 65
9 The "Sixties Scoop" 71
10 The Indigenous child removal system in Canada 79
11 Suicide 87
12 Missing and Murdered Indigenous Women 91
13 "Starlight Tours" 95

| Legislation, Reports, and Inquiries 99
14 | Highlights from the Indian Act 101
15 | UN Report on Indigenous Rights 107
16 | The White Paper 1969 109
17 | The Red Paper 113
18 | Truth and Reconciliation 117
19 | Empty Apologies? 143
20 | Conclusion 157
21 | Bibliography 159

For My Daughters,
Who inspire me to try and leave the
world a little better than I found it…

Copyright @2024 by Adultbrain Publishing
All rights reserved
Published in Canada by Adultbrain Publishing
Www.adultbrain.ca
adultBrain books are available at large quantity special discounts. signed copies and audio versions may also be available. For more information contact publishing@adultbrain.ca
Grimes, Darren
A Canadian Shame: The Indian Act and Residential Schools / by Darren Grimes

ISBN - 978-1-0690495-0-6
eISBN - 978-1-0690495-1-3
Text Design: Natascha van Tonder
Jacket Art: Natascha van Tonder
Editing: Natascha van Tonder
2nd Edition
Special Thanks:
Graham Dunlop
David Mathisen
Mom
My Daughters

Website:
ACanadianShame.ca

Foreword

Long ago, according to a sacred story preserved by the Tlingit people, there lived a terrible giant whose most noteworthy characteristic was his appetite for the consumption of mortal men and women. This giant craved human flesh for his food, and human blood for his drink.

The story, originally written down in 1883, is recounted in American Indian Myths and Legends, published in 1984 and edited by Richard Erdoes and Alfonso Ortiz (and can be found on pages 191 through 193). In the story, we learn that the giant has a special fondness for roasting and devouring human hearts. The monster is so successful at capturing the people in order to make them into his meals that a special council is convened to discuss the situation:

"Unless we can get rid of this giant," the people said, "none of us will be left," (Erdoes & Ortiz, 1984, p 191)

We might think that the people would have called a counsel and determined a way to stop the giant before the crisis reached such a dire state that their complete extermination was imminent – but perhaps at first those who had not yet fallen victim to the giant did not want to face the obvious but terrifying fact that a giant with a taste for human flesh, human blood, and human hearts was not likely to stop devouring men and women until all of them had become his food and drink.

In A Canadian Shame, Darren Grimes has collected and presented overwhelming evidence which shows beyond doubt that a monster bent on the complete destruction of the Indigenous peoples of Canada –

First Nations, Inuit, Metis, and all the other Aboriginal inhabitants of the land – that has been devouring not only men and women, but also children of those cultures, that this monster has been doing so for hundreds of years, that this destruction has been deliberate, and systematic rather than accidental or unintended, and that lethal aspects of this horrifying feeding frenzy continue right up to the present day.

In this book you will encounter the record of the residential schools, established in the 1880s and placed under the control of various Christian church organizations, where children from Native families were taken against their parents' will, and where those children were deliberately exposed to tuberculosis, this fact being substantiated by countless eyewitness accounts, including by conscientious doctors from previous centuries who complained about what they were seeing, as well as being substantiated by photographs showing obviously sick children dining with and rooming with healthy children – some being forced to sleep in the same beds with children who already had the disease – and who were given substandard medical care (in accordance with written policy).

We do not know how many died, because this genocidal policy was deliberately covered up (with government document-destruction teams obliterating countless records at the Residential Schools prior to their eventual closure) and its perpetrators allowed to operate without any accountability – but in recent months, massive numbers of unmarked graves are being discovered at the sites of former residential schools, unmarked remains numbering into the several hundreds of victims at some locations. The sheer magnitude of the findings, and the fact that they remained unreported and unexamined all the way until this very year makes it difficult to argue that this atrocity was anything other than a deliberate and diabolical policy, and one that was not isolated to a single residential school but rather was carried out across the board.

You will read of the ongoing work of Kevin Daniel Annett, who first became aware of the legacy of the residential schools in the early 1990s as an ordained minister in the United Church of Canada, his awareness sparked by the stories he began hearing from many Native men and women during the course of performing his ministry. When Kevin Annett began to call attention to the size and scope of the problem, he found himself summarily fired by the church without cause or notice in 1995. The first books he wrote exposing the horrendous history he was uncovering were taken out of print by his publishers: he subsequently made all of his work available online for free.

What do the actions taken against Kevin Annett by the Church of Canada and by his publishers indicate about the continuing strength of this giant which has already devoured so many? And in this present book by Darren Grimes, you will also find accounts of records of investigations into mysterious Native deaths being "destroyed during a routine purge of old files" – as recently as 1998.

In this present book A Canadian Shame, you will also encounter the stomach-turning policy of involuntary sterilization of countless Native children consigned to the residential schools, a policy that was formally passed by legislatures in Canada, allowing any inmate of any residential school to be forcibly sterilized at the decision of the school's principal (who were employees of the churches running the schools). This sterilization was typically done by exposing the child's pelvic region to x-ray machines for extended periods of time – and this practice (which was established by legislative motion beginning in 1929) continued all the way up through the 1980s.

You will also learn that Native children were used in medical experiments before, during, and even after World War II – experiments which included deliberate starvation, drug testing for a variety of reasons including "behavior modification," experiments to study "pain thresholds," experiments for the testing of chemical weapons, and experiments involving different methods of sterilization. These tests were done at the residential schools, as well as at military bases and in special laboratories and "Indian hospitals run jointly with the United, Anglican and Catholic churches" (p48). Clearly, such experiments are immoral, illegal, and constitute atrocious violations of human rights. They continued for decades after World War II -- decades after the Nuremberg trials and the Nuremberg Code which was created in 1947 as a reaction to the human experimentation perpetrated by the Nazis.

You will learn about the criminal institution which became known as the "Sixties Scoop," which allowed children of Native families to be literally abducted by "child welfare" agencies and placed into foster families under new non-Native "parents," a policy which began in the late 1950s as some of the residential schools began to be shut down and which basically served as a new and decentralized version of the same culture-destroying policy, one which continued into the 1980s.

You will learn about a history of different sets of laws for Native and non-Native men and women in Canada, including restrictions on voting, on movement (passes being required to leave reservations), even restrictions on rights to legal counsel and the specific forbidding of lawyers representing Natives in cases involving land disagreements.

And you will learn that, despite the fact that the most overt and egregious of these institutions from previous decades have now ended, the government of Canada to this day still fails to provide clean and safe drinking water to all of the First Nations reserves. Statistics show unequivocally that men and women of Indigenous descent suffer far higher levels of poverty, unemployment, incarceration, addiction, depression, and suicide than non-Native populations in Canada – undoubtedly as a result of the genocidal policies discussed above, as well as the ongoing failure of the government to properly provide infrastructure to serve all the people equally, as well as by the ongoing lack of justice and accountability for crimes against men and women of Indigenous heritage which can be seen from examples given in this book.

And while the genocidal measures described above (more of which you will encounter as your read A Canadian Shame) have been particularly atrocious in Canada, this problem is obviously not confined to Canada alone. Similar policies were of course carried out in the United States, and throughout the rest of the Americas – and stretch back to the 1500s.

Indeed, as I write in my 2014 book The Undying Stars, there is reason to suspect that the violence which would be inflicted upon the men and women of the Americas may have been part of "some kind of standing order that had been given to the leaders of the expedition, before they ever left the shores of Europe," pointing to evidence that Columbus possessed "portolan" style maps showing the location and outlines of the Americas before he ever set sail, and arguing that, "The wholesale destruction of the written texts of the Maya, the constant accompaniment of the priests in the entire procedure, and the careful recording of the results (again by the priests) suggests that something more was at work here" (342 – 343).

The outsized role played by Christian churches (of various denominations) in the hideous and inhuman residential school industry of Canada – where we find inescapable evidence of deliberate medical neglect, along with rampant physical abuse, mental abuse, and sexual abuse as described by too many survivors of the residential system, as well as the criminal medical experimentation described above, the implementation of forced sterilization, and the cover-up of currently-unknown numbers of deaths of children whose remains are now being discovered in fields of unmarked graves – also leads to the inescapable conclusion that "something more is at work here." If we read the evidence carefully, we see the indications of an implacable enemy which had already been devouring hearts in other parts of the globe before it arrived on the shores of the Americas.

Without minimizing the horror of the crimes perpetrated against the Native population of Canada (and the rest of the Americas) in any way, we can note the undeniable fact that forced medical experimentation (including forced sterilization) was also perpetrated on the victims of the Holocaust in World War II, as well as on thousands of men and women of all ethnic backgrounds (but almost always of the most exploited socio-economic classes) in the United States prior to World War II, and even afterwards. And we see hints of the same pitiless criminality in programs such as the MKULTRA mind control experiments which were carried out during the Cold War (again, long after the adoption of the Nuremberg Code).

As you will see in the pages that follow (and as Kevin Annett has documented using accounts from survivors), German-speaking doctors came to Canada in the 1930s to supervise and direct some of the experiments carried out on children of Indigenous heritage prior to World War II, and even afterwards – including experiments supervised by suspected members of the Nazi SS during the decades after the formal cessation of that war in 1945, many of whom were brought to the US and Canada during Operation Paperclip.

The evidence contained in the pages that follow provides all the bread crumbs anyone needs for reaching the conclusion that the pattern of horrific policies that unfolded in Canada was not the result of positive or well-intentioned ideas that "just went wrong" because of incompetence or venality. Nor can we conclude that all of the shocking crimes detailed in this book were "just" the result of racist ideas that prevailed at the time and have since been corrected. In fact, we see that doctors from more than a hundred years ago who visited the residential schools within just a few years of their being created were already shocked and appalled at the medical neglect and deliberate exposure to tuberculosis they were seeing on a widespread basis, and they took steps to try to inform the proper authorities in order to correct the situation – only to discover that the authorities obviously knew what was going on and supported the unethical practices. The trauma being inflicted on the Native population (not only upon the children, of course, but also upon their parents) was deliberate: it was the plan, not a failure of the plan.

Those doctors in the late 1800s and early 1900s may not have realized it, but they were encountering a monster that was already busy trying to devour the whole world. Certainly the horror it was inflicting upon the First Nations and Aboriginal people of Canada was appalling, as you will see from the pages of this book – but these atrocities fit into a pattern of a world-devouring giant which seeks to take the resources of all people everywhere, while devouring their flesh, drinking their blood, roasting their hearts for dessert, and casting what's left upon the rubbish pile.

This monster will not stop until men and women, like those people long ago described in the story of the Tlingit, are ready to actually admit to the existence of the problem, and to realize that what is happening is not going to stop by itself.

Obviously, the Indigenous people already know all too well what is going on – they know that a terrible giant has been mercilessly devouring the flesh and drinking the blood of their people for too long -- but all the people of the world need to wake up to the same threat, because it will not confine its attentions only to Canada, nor will it only seek to devour the members of the First Nations. A giant that will perform the kinds of acts listed in this book must be seen for what it is. Everyone everywhere is in the position of the men and women in the Tlingit story, who declare that "Unless we can get rid of this giant, none of us will be left."

In that story, one brave member of the people takes it upon himself to confront the giant. Feigning death, the man lies in the path where the giant is sure to come by. Picking up the man and finding he is still warm and fresh, the giant congratulates himself and throws the man over his back, taking him back to the giant's lair. There, the man finds out where the giant's heart is located – in the giant's left heel. Taking the giant's own enormous skinning knife, the brave man plunges it into the giant's heel, causing all the monster's life-blood to rush out.

Like virtually all of the world's ancient myths, from cultures around the globe (including the stories collected into what we call the Bible), this Tlingit story can be seen to be based on celestial metaphor. A giant who is defeated by draining the blood in his heel is undoubtedly based upon the constellation Orion, a towering figure in the night sky and one whose left foot (marked by the bright star Rigel) is immediately adjacent to the long and winding constellation known as the River Eridanus:

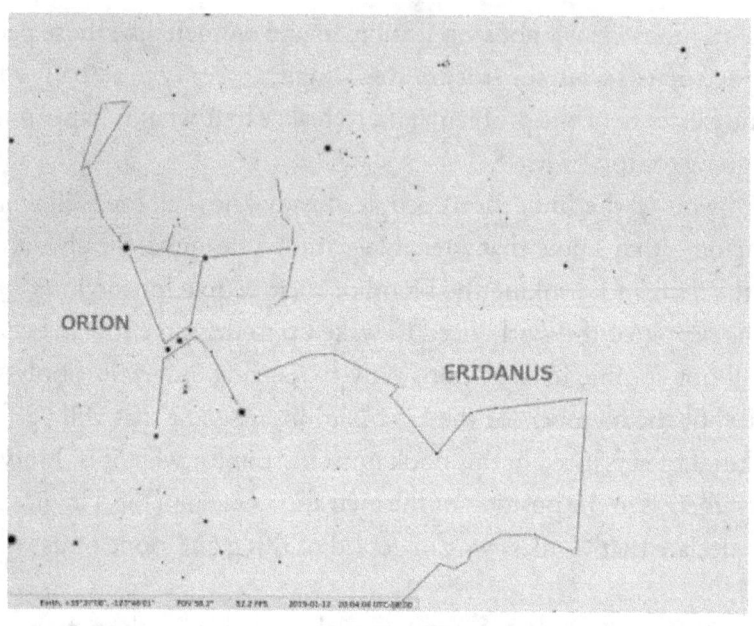

RIGEL

It takes only a little effort to see that we can envision an additional "connecting line" from the start of the River Eridanus (just above Orion's foot) and the star Rigel in Orion – and thus to envision Eridanus flowing out of Orion's foot. And, note that the Tlingit story specifies that it is the giant's left heel where his heart is located: if we envision Orion as a giant which is facing us, then foot closest to Eridanus, and the foot marked by the bright star Rigel, would be the left foot of Orion (the very foot from which the blood of the giant flows out).

It is no coincidence that in the myths of ancient Greece there is another giant who is put out of commission in a similar manner: the bronze giant Talos, which guards the shores of Crete. According to one myth, there was a screw in the heel of this bronze giant, and when that screw was removed, the ichor which animated the marvelous mechanical man all flowed out upon the ground, resulting in the demise of Talos.

Also, I have argued in the past that the "foot-washing scenes" found in both the climactic chapters of the Odyssey of ancient Greece and in the gospel texts included in the New Testament canon are also almost certainly based upon the part of the night sky in which the River Eridanus can be seen to be flowing "out of"— or at least adjacent to – the foot of Orion.

In the Tlingit story, however, the victory over the giant is short-lived. As the blood runs out of the heel-wound, the giant informs his attacker that he will never stop drinking the blood of human men and women, even in death. The man, in order to try to prevent such an outcome, chops up the body of the giant, and throws all the pieces into the fire. The man then takes the ashes and scatters them into the air for the winds to blow away.

As the man does so, the cloud of ashes is transformed into a cloud of mosquitos – and from the cloud of insects, the man can hear the giant's voice laughing at him, and saying "Yes, I'll eat you people until the end of time" (Erdoes & Ortiz, 1984, p 193).

And so we see that the solution to the problem is not straightforward, and it is certainly not easy. It will require courage, certainly, as demonstrated in the Tlingit legend – but it will also require careful consideration, so that one form of the giant does not simply mutate into another.

But the first step is to realize that the problem exists – it is not something that only belongs to the past, it is not something that just happened by accident or happened "in spite of all good intentions," and it is something which threatens all of humanity. This book by Darren Grimes provides all the evidence that is needed for us to see it, and to tell others about it.

Because unless we start to see it, and figure out what to do about it, "none of us will be left."

David W. Mathisen
Paso Robles, California
18 July, 2021

2

Preface

Canadian kindness and hospitality are attributes celebrated around the globe, many hailing it as one of the most free, fair, and diverse societies in the Western world today. But it is one with an ugly secret, and an even uglier past. Recently Canada fell short on a UN Security Council seat for a failure to act abroad on human rights.

New Democratic Party (NDP) foreign affairs critic Jack Harris called the defeat "very disappointing" and said Canada's contributions to developmental assistance, peacekeeping, climate change, and Indigenous rights were likely factors.

"What is more, we have been inconsistent in our support for human rights, going so far as to vote against almost every UN resolution upholding Palestinian rights and signing a new arms export agreement with Saudi Arabia, despite their egregious human rights abuses," he said.
(Harris, 2020)

Furthermore, Canada was one of only four countries to vote no on The United Nations Declaration on the Rights of Indigenous Peoples in 2007, with 144 countries voting yes. Canada's co-conspirators in continuing international denial of Indigenous rights at home were the United States, Australia and New Zealand. Though the declaration had widespread support from the international community, the Canadian government had this to say:

In his address to the General Assembly before the vote, Canada's UN ambassador, John McNee, said Canada had "significant concerns" over the declaration's wording on provisions addressing lands and resources, as well as another article calling on states to obtain prior informed consent with indigenous groups before enacting new laws or administrative measures.

Article 26 of the UN declaration states: "Indigenous peoples have the right to the lands, territories and resources which they have traditionally owned, occupied or otherwise used or acquired."

McNee said the provision is "overly broad, unclear and capable of a wide variety of interpretations" that could lead to the reopening of previously settled land claims and existing treaties.
("Canada votes 'no' as UN native rights declaration passes", 2007)

The ironic thing about existing land claims and treaties is that they seem to matter little when a new highway, railway or pipeline is required. Furthermore, under the Indian Act, First Nations people do not own their own land. Instead it is held for them by the government, a little known fact among the public today. For the first half of the 20th century, Canadian law allowed for uncultivated reserve lands to be leased off to settlers at the government's discretion, land that in many cases would never find its way back into Indigenous hands. Canadian law also dictated under the Indian Act that Indian Reserves were a nuisance to expanding towns, and thus could be relocated at the government's sole discretion without the input of the Indian band, should a town grow to a population of more than 8,000 people in the vicinity of the reserve lands.

Recent discoveries of mass unmarked graves at old residential school sites in Canada has led to a recent interest in the history of the schools and, by association, the other forms of legislated cultural, and arguably actual, genocidal acts by the Canadian government. The Indian Act still exists in Canada today. I am a Registered Indian with the Mishkeegogamang band. This comes with an identification card and a registration number, as well as some benefits like access to free dental services and medical prescriptions. Some bands offer free tuition for post-secondary education as well. A common misconception is that Indigenous Canadians do not have to pay tax, but this is only the case if you work on a reserve.

The Canadian government website hosts the Indian Act in its current form, as well as all the amendments dating back to the early 2000's. While the Act itself has been in existence for 154 years, the earlier most atrocious versions of the legislation have seemingly been removed from the official website. It does still exist on some First Nation's community websites, and it can still be downloaded from here,
http://kopiwadan.ca/honesty/indian-act/?lang=en

This book is an attempt to pull together the over 150-year history of the Indian Act in Canada, and the damage it has caused to generations of Indigenous families across the country, and which continues to do so to this day. From genocidal legislation and state-sponsored assimilation, to apologies and attempts at reconciliation, I attempt to do so in a length that is not too overwhelming to the reader. What follows is a collection of quotes, legislation, reports, timelines, and articles that hope to bring the reader up to speed on a century and a half of the Indigenous experience in the Great White North. Here are just a few of the sections of the Indian Act, or policies that were particularly oppressive and destructive to a people and their culture:

- Ban of religious ceremonies like the Potlatch
- Ban of Indians leaving Reserves without Indian Agent Permission
- Inability of Indians to vote
- Introduction of Mandatory Residential Schools
- Denial of status of Indian women
- Creation of Reserves
- Prohibition of sale of alcohol
- Prohibition of sale of ammunition
- Prohibition of Solicitation of funds for Indian legal claims

These are only a few of the atrocities hidden within the Indian Act over its century and a half long existence, a document that is still legally binding at the time of this writing (2021). This book hopes to preserve all the iterations of this historically important piece of legislation.

At the time of this writing, several bands from around Canada have been finding the mass and unmarked graves of children nearby historic residential school sites throughout Canada, including but not limited to:

- 215 bodies at Kamloops Indian Residential School
- 109 bodies at the Brandon Indian residential School
- 751 bodies at the Marieval Indian Residential School

This book hopes to serve as a brief historical record of the relationship between the Canadian government, the Church, and the Indigenous Peoples of Canada, in an effort to make sure that the crimes of the past are not forgotten so that true reconciliation can be part of our future.

Miigwech,
Darren Grimes
Waabishki-Ma'iingan

3

Definitions

From the Indian Act of 1985
2 (1) In this Act,
band means a body of Indians
(a) for whose use and benefit in common, lands, the legal title to which is vested in Her Majesty, have been set apart before, on or after September 4, 1951,
(b) for whose use and benefit in common, moneys are held by Her Majesty, or
(c) declared by the Governor in Council to be a band for the purposes of this Act; (bande)
band list means a list of persons that is maintained under section 8 by a band or in the Department; (liste de bande)
child includes a legally adopted child and a child adopted in accordance with Indian custom; (enfant)
common-law partner, in relation to an individual, means a person who is cohabiting with the individual in a conjugal relationship, having so cohabited for a period of at least one year; (conjoint de fait)
council of the band means
(a) in the case of a band to which section 74 applies, the council established pursuant to that section,
(b) in the case of a band that is named in the schedule to the First Nations Elections Act, the council elected or in office in accordance with that Act,

(c) in the case of a band whose name has been removed from the schedule to the First Nations Elections Act in accordance with section 42 of that Act, the council elected or in office in accordance with the community election code referred to in that section, or

(d) in the case of any other band, the council chosen according to the custom of the band, or, if there is no council, the chief of the band chosen according to the custom of the band; (conseil de la bande)

department means the Department of Indigenous Services; (ministère)

designated lands means a tract of land or any interest therein the legal title to which remains vested in Her Majesty and in which the band for whose use and benefit it was set apart as a reserve has, otherwise than absolutely, released or surrendered its rights or interests, whether before or after the coming into force of this definition; (terres désignées)

elector means a person who

(a) is registered on a Band List,

(b) is of the full age of eighteen years, and

(c) is not disqualified from voting at band elections; (électeur)

estate includes real and personal property and any interest in land; (biens)

Indian means a person who pursuant to this Act is registered as an Indian or is entitled to be registered as an Indian; (Indien)

Indian moneys means all moneys collected, received or held by Her Majesty for the use and benefit of Indians or bands; (argent des Indiens)

Indian Register means the register of persons that is maintained under section 5; (registre des Indiens)

intoxicant includes alcohol, alcoholic, spirituous, vinous, fermented malt or other intoxicating liquor or combination of liquors and mixed liquor a part of which is spirituous, vinous, fermented or otherwise intoxicating and all drinks, drinkable liquids, preparations or mixtures capable of human consumption that are intoxicating; (boisson alcoolisée) member of a band means a person whose name appears on a Band List or who is entitled to have his name appear on a Band List; (membre d'une bande)

mentally incompetent Indian means an Indian who, pursuant to the laws of the province in which he resides, has been found to be mentally defective or incompetent for the purposes of any laws of that province providing for the administration of estates of mentally defective or incompetent persons; (Indien mentalement incapable)

Minister means the Minister of Indigenous Services; (ministre)

registered means registered as an Indian in the Indian Register; (inscrit)

Registrar means the officer in the Department who is in charge of the Indian Register and the Band Lists maintained in the Department; (registraire)

reserve

(a) means a tract of land, the legal title to which is vested in Her Majesty, that has been set apart by Her Majesty for the use and benefit of a band, and

(b) except in subsection 18(2), sections 20 to 25, 28, 37, 38, 42, 44, 46, 48 to 51 and 58 to 60 and the regulations made under any of those provisions, includes designated lands; (réserve)

superintendent includes a commissioner, regional supervisor, Indian superintendent, assistant Indian superintendent and any other person declared by the Minister to be a superintendent for the purposes of this Act, and with reference to a band or a reserve, means the superintendent for that band or reserve; (surintendant)

surrendered lands means a reserve or part of a reserve or any interest therein, the legal title to which remains vested in Her Majesty, that has been released or surrendered by the band for whose use and benefit it was set apart; (terres cédées)

survivor, in relation to a deceased individual, means their surviving spouse or common-law partner. (survivant)

(Indian Act, 1985)

4

Notable Players

Sir John A Macdonald,
1st Prime Minister of Canada.
Architect of the Indian Act

AN 1888 CARTOON FROM THE NOWDEFUNCT GRIP MAGAZINE SHOWING MACDONALD AND INDIAN COMMISSIONER EDGAR DEWDNEY

Sir John Alexander Macdonald was the first prime minister of Canada. The dominant figure of Canadian Confederation, he had a political career that spanned almost half a century. Macdonald was born in Scotland; when he was a boy his family immigrated to Kingston in the Province of Upper Canada. As the architect of the Indian Act, his opinions of the Indigenous population are important, dated or not. Here are a few of his quotes on Indigenous People.

"to wean them by slow degrees, from their nomadic habits, which have almost become an instinct, and by slow degrees absorb them or settle them on the land. Meantime they must be fairly protected. " (Biggar, 1985. P. 177)

"When the school is on the reserve, the child lives with its parents, who are savages, and though he may learn to read and write, his habits and training mode of thought are Indian. He is simply a savage who can read and write. It has been strongly impressed upon myself, as head of the Department, that Indian children should be withdrawn as much as possible from the parental influence, and the only way to do that would be to put them in central training industrial schools where they will acquire the habits and modes of thought of white men." (House of Commons Debates, 1883. p1107–1108)

"I have reason to believe that the agents as a whole ... are doing all they can, by refusing food until the Indians are on the verge of starvation, to reduce the expense," (House of Commons Debates, 1882. p. 1186)

Duncan Campbell Scott
Deputy Superintendent General of Indian Affairs from 1913 – 1932 and Poet

The Half-Breed Girl
by Duncan Campbell Scott
She is free of the trap and the paddle,
The portage and the trail,
But something behind her savage life
Shines like a fragile veil.
Her dreams are undiscovered,
Shadows trouble her breast,
When the time for resting cometh
Then least is she at rest.
Oft in the morns of winter,
When she visits the rabbit snares,

An appearance floats in the crystal air
Beyond the balsam firs.
Oft in the summer mornings
When she strips the nets of fish,
The smell of the dripping net-twine
Gives to her heart a wish.
But she cannot learn the meaning
Of the shadows in her soul,
The lights that break and gather,
The clouds that part and roll,
The reek of rock-built cities,
Where her fathers dwelt of yore,
The gleam of loch and shealing,
The mist on the moor,
Frail traces of kindred kindness,
Of feud by hill and strand,
The heritage of an age-long life
In a legendary land.
She wakes in the stifling wigwam,
Where the air is heavy and wild,
She fears for something or nothing
With the heart of a frightened child.
She sees the stars turn slowly
Past the tangle of the poles,
Through the smoke of the dying embers,
Like the eyes of dead souls.
Her heart is shaken with longing
For the strange, still years,
For what she knows and knows not,
For the wells of ancient tears.
A voice calls from the rapids,
Deep, careless and free,
A voice that is larger than her life

> Or than her death shall be.
> She covers her face with her blanket,
> Her fierce soul hates her breath,
> As it cries with a sudden passion
> For life or death.
> (Scott, 1926. P55-56)

While somewhat less poetic, here a few more quotes from Mr Scott.

"It has always been clear to me that the Indians must have some sort of recreation, and if our agents would endeavor to substitute reasonable amusements for this senseless drumming and dancing, it would be a great assistance." (Titley, 1986. p. 177)

"I want to get rid of the Indian problem.....Our objective is to continue until there is not an Indian that has not been absorbed into the body politic, and there is no Indian question, and no Indian Department..." (Scott, 1920. National Archives of Canada)

"...the system was open to criticism. Insufficient care was exercised in the admission of children to the schools. The well-known predisposition of Indians to tuberculosis resulted in a very large percentage of deaths among the pupils. They were housed in buildings not carefully designed for school purposes, and these buildings became infected and dangerous to the inmates. It is quite within the mark to say that fifty per cent of the children who passed through these schools did not live to benefit from the education which they had received therein." (TRC Canada, 2015, p. 375)

Peter Henderson Bryce
   Chief Medical Officer of the federal Department of Immigration 1904

THE STORY
OF
A NATIONAL CRIME

BY
P. H. BRYCE, M.A., M.D.
BEING

AN APPEAL FOR JUSTICE
TO THE
INDIANS OF CANADA

The Wards of the Nation:
Our Allies in the Revolutionary War:
Our Brothers-in-Arms in the Great War.

Peter Henderson Bryce became an ally to Canada's Indigenous People shortly after becoming the first Chief Medical Officer of the Interior in 1904, twenty years after the start of mandatory residential school enrolment. Tasked with "systematic collection of health statistics of the several hundred Indian bands scattered over Canada" (Bryce, 1922).

In 1907 he reported that over 25% of the (1537) students had died from tuberculosis, with some schools approaching 70% death rates. Bryce's report blamed school construction and care standards for the much higher rates of TB in the schools which went against the popular racial susceptibility theory of the time. (Bryce, 1907)

Bryce wrote that Indigenous children enrolled in residential schools were deprived of adequate medical attention and sanitary living conditions. He suggested improvements to national policies regarding the care and education of Indigenous peoples that would drastically reduce TB rates in the schools, however all of them were rejected as "too costly" and the report never went public. In 1921 Bryce was forced into retirement by government and although he appealed the decision, he was ultimately denied. Shortly after his forced resignation he published his earlier suppressed report condemning the treatment of the Indigenous at the hands of the British North America Act.

Timelines

5

Timeline of The Indian Act

The following timeline can be found at https://www.nwac.ca/wp-content/uploads/2018/04/The-Indian-Act-Said-WHAT-pdf-1.pdf

- 1876-Present
- 1876 - The Indian Act is created. Any existing Indigenous self-government structures at this time are extinguished.
- 1880 - Though not a law but a policy, Indigenous farmers are expected to have a permit to sell cattle, grain, hay, or produce. They must also have a permit to buy groceries and clothes.
- 1884 - Attendance in residential schools becomes mandatory for status Indians until the age of sixteen. Children are forcibly removed and separated from their families and are not allowed to speak their own language or practice their own religious rituals. The sale of alcohol to Indigenous peoples is prohibited
- 1885 - Indigenous peoples are banned from conducting their own spiritual ceremonies such as the potlatch. A pass system is also created and Indigenous peoples are restricted from leaving their reserve without permission.
- 1886 - The definition of Indian is expanded to include "any person who is reputed to belong to a particular band or who follows the Indian mode of life, or any child of such person." Vol-

untary enfranchisement is allowed for anyone who is "of good moral character" and "temperate in his or her habits".
- 1914 - Indigenous peoples are required to ask for official permission before wearing any "costume" (traditional attire) at public events. Dancing is out-lawed off reserve. In 1925, it is outlawed entirely.
- 1918 - The Canadian government gives itself the power to lease out Indigenous land to non-Indigenous persons if it is not being used for farming.
- 1927 - Indigenous peoples are banned from hiring lawyers or legal representation regarding land claims against the federal government without the government's approval.
- 1951 - After the Joint Committee of the Senate and House of Commons are-examines the Act again in the late 1940's, the bans on dances, ceremonies, and legal claims are removed. Women are now allowed to vote in band council elections. Provisions that are still in place include compulsory enfranchisement through marriage to a non-status man; Indigenous peoples who receive a degree or become a doctor, clergyman or lawyer lose status. 1951 amendments now enact the "double mother rule" which removes the status of a person whose mother and grandmother were given status through marriage.
- 1960 - Indigenous peoples are finally allowed to vote in federal elections. That is to say, for nearly a century, Indigenous peoples were denied the right to vote for the government that had stolen their land from them.
- 1961 - Compulsory enfranchisement is removed.
- 1969 - The first Trudeau government announces its intentions to entirely eliminate the Indian Act with the White Paper. This draws great ire from Indigenous communities and the government abandons the idea.

- 1970 - The Royal Commission on the Status of Women recommends that legislation be enacted to repeal sexist Indian Act provisions.
- 1973 - The Supreme Court rules that Indigenous rights to land do indeed exist and cites the 1763 Royal Proclamation as proof. This translates into an actual victory in the following decade, when the Inuvialuit Claims Settlement Act comes into force in 1984, giving Inuit of the western Arctic control over resources.
- 1978 - Canada issues a report which acknowledges the sexist marrying out rule which strips status women of their status and benefits if they marry non-status men. Sandra Lovelace challenges this rule in the late 1970s, petitioning to the UN Human Rights Committee in her quest. In 1981, the committee finds that the loss of a woman's status upon marriage violates the International Covenant on Civil and Political Rights.
- 1985 - Bill C-31 comes into effect. The marrying out rule in the Indian Act is finally removed but further distinctions in status are created, with additional issues stemming from this distinction. Re-instated women are given status, while men retain status.

6

Residential Schools

In Canada, the Indian residential school system was a network of mandatory boarding schools for Indigenous peoples. The network was funded by the Canadian government's Department of Indian Affairs and administered by Christian churches. The school system was created to remove Indigenous children from the influence of their own culture and assimilate them into the dominant European-Canadian culture. Over the course of the system's more than hundred-year existence, at least 150,000 children were placed in residential schools nationally. By the 1930s about 30 percent of Indigenous children were believed to be attending residential schools. The number of school-related deaths remains unknown due to incomplete records. Estimates range from 3,200 to over 30,000.

Indian Residential Schools – Chronology

Placed with permission. John Edmond is an Ottawa lawyer with an interest in constitutional and Aboriginal law. He is a member of the bars of Ontario and British Columbia, and served as Commission Counsel to the Indian Claims Commission 2003-08. The chronology can be found at

https://www.lawnow.org/indian-residential-schools-chronology/

This chronology was compiled to convey, by historic milestones, how the Indian Residential School system came to be, how it embodied attitudes of its time, how critics were dismissed, and how finally the deep harm it did to many members of generations of Indian children was exposed in the course of a reconciliation process that continues.

While Canada has apologized and provided compensation, much of the damage to individuals, and to First Nations culture, can never be put right.

This first appeared in LawNow magazine in 2014. A version updated to 2017 was published as Appendix 2 to 21 things you may not know about the Indian Act (Indigenous Relations Press, 2018). This is essentially that version, so does not include more recent events, such as the tragic discoveries of graves near schools. ©John Edmond

- 1755 – Indian Department created as branch of British military to establish and maintain relations with Indians.

- 1820 – This decade sees Anglican and Methodist missionary schools established in Upper Canada and Red River settlement.

- 1842 – Governor General Sir Charles Bagot appoints Commission to report on "the Affairs of the Indians in Canada."

- 1844 – Bagot Commission finds reserve communities in a "half-civilized state"; recommends assimilationist policy, including establishment of boarding schools distant from child's community, to provide training in manual labour and agriculture; portends major shift away from Royal Proclamation of 1763 policy that Indians were autonomous entities under Crown protection.

- 1847 – Dr. Adolphus Egerton Ryerson, Methodist minister and educational reformer, commissioned by Assistant Superintendent General of Indian Affairs to study Native education, supports Bagot approach (as does Governor General Lord Elgin); proposes model on which Indian Residential School system was built.

- 1856 – "Any hope of raising the Indians ... to the ... level of their white neighbours, is yet a ... distant spark": Governor General Sir Edmund Head's Commission "to Investigate Indian Affairs in Canada."

- 1857 – Gradual Civilization Act passed; males "sufficiently advanced in the elementary branches of education" could be enfranchised (they would no longer be "Indians," and could vote).

- 1861 – St. Mary's Mission Indian Residential School, Mission, and Presbyterian Coqualeetza Indian Residential School, Chilliwack, first residential schools in B.C., established.

- 1862 – What became Blue Quills Indian Residential School (Hospice of St. Joseph / Lac la Biche Boarding School) established at Lac la Biche, later Saddle Lake, then St. Paul, AB; first residential school on the Prairies.

- 1867 – Confederation: British North America Act (now Constitution Act, 1867) establishes federal jurisdiction over Indians. Thus, while education is under provincial jurisdiction, Indian matters including education are federal.
Fort Providence and Fort Resolution Indian Residential Schools established; first residential schools north of 60°.

- 1871 – Treaty No. 1 entered into at Lower Fort Garry: "Her Majesty agrees to maintain a school on each reserve ... whenever the Indians of the reserve should desire it." This promise, repeated in subsequent treaties (though hedged in Treaties No. 5 on), reflected desire of Indian leadership to ensure transition of their youth to demands of anticipated newcomer society.

-

- 1876 – Indian Act passed into law by Parliament.

- 1879 – Nicholas Flood Davin, journalist and defeated Tory candidate, commissioned by Prime Minister Macdonald, also Minister of the Interior, to produce proposal for Indian education; visits US industrial schools grounded in policy of "aggressive civilization"; produces Report on Industrial Schools for Indians and Half-Breeds. Four residential schools already operated in Ontario; "mission schools" planned for the west. This date generally taken to mark beginning of Indian Residential Schools, though the system had early predecessors in New France and New Brunswick, and several schools were already operating.
Duncan Campbell Scott, best known later as a "Confederation poet," joins Indian Affairs at age 17 as "copying clerk," at direction of Macdonald.

- 1883 – First industrial school established, at Battleford, modelled on Davin Report.

- 1885 – Residential schools necessary to remove children from influence of the home only way "of advancing the Indian in civilization": Lawrence Vankoughnet, Deputy Superintendent General, to Prime Minister Macdonald. Despite treaty promises, reserves lacked schools; removal, often forcible, of pupils to residential schools is option chosen by government.

- 1890 – Physician Dr. G. Orton reports to Indian Affairs that tuberculosis in the schools could be reduced by half; measures rejected as "too costly."

- 1892 – Regulations passed giving control over daily school administration to churches: Catholic, Anglican, Presbyterian,

Methodist. (In 1925, Methodists joined most Presbyterians and others to form United Church, which continued to run schools.)

- 1896 – Programme of Studies issued; stresses importance of replacing "native tongue" with English. Children forbidden to speak their native language, even to each other, and punished for doing so. This continued to be the policy for life of the system.

- 1904 – Dr. Peter Bryce appointed "Medical Inspector" to the Departments of the Interior and Indian Affairs.

- 1904 – Minister Sir Clifford Sifton announces closure of industrial schools – large urban institutions – in favour of boarding schools. They are closed over the next two decades.

- 1907 – Dr. Bryce visits 35 schools; reports appallingly unsanitary conditions, micro-organism- bearing ventilation, high death rates; "the almost invariable cause" is tuberculosis.
"The appalling number of deaths among the younger children ... brings the Department within unpleasant nearness to the charge of manslaughter": Hon. S.H. Blake, K.C., Chair of Advisory Board on Indian Education (partner in what is now national law firm Blake, Cassels & Graydon), to Minister Frank Oliver.

- 1908 – Indian Affairs Accountant F.H. Paget reports school buildings in bad condition. 1909 – Duncan Campbell Scott appointed Superintendent of Indian Education.

- 1910 – "I can safely say that barely half of the children in our Indian schools survive to take advantage of the education we are offering them": Scott to Major D.M. McKay, Indian Affairs

Agent General in B.C.

The children "catch the disease … in a building … burdened with Tuberculosis Bacilli": Duck Lake Indian Agent MacArthur on the continuing prevalence of tuberculosis.

- 1912 – "… in the early days of school administration … [t]he well-known predisposition of
Indians to tuberculosis resulted in a very large percentage of deaths among the pupils … fifty percent of the children who passed through these schools did not live to benefit from the education which they had received therein": Scott, in an essay in the authoritative 22-volume Canada and its Provinces.

- 1913 – Scott appointed Deputy Superintendent General of Indian Affairs (deputy minister), reporting to Minister of the Interior and Superintendent General Dr. William A. Roche.

- 1919 – Position of Medical Inspector for Indian Agencies and Residential Schools abolished (in the year of the Spanish 'flu) by order in council on recommendation of Scott "for reasons of economy."

- 1920 – "I want to get rid of the Indian problem": D.C. Scott to Parliamentary Committee. A Scott-instigated amendment to the Indian Act, with church concurrence, compelled school attendance of all children aged seven to fifteen. Though no particular kind of school was stipulated, Scott favoured residential schooling to eliminate the influences of home and reserve and hasten assimilation.

"I am afraid I cannot give a very encouraging answer to the question. We are not convinced that it is increasing, but it is not decreasing": Prime Minister Arthur Meighen, former Ministerof the Interior, on being asked whether tuberculosis was increasing or decreasing amongst the Indians.

- 1922 – Dr. Bryce publishes The Story of a National Crime: Being an Appeal for Justice to the Indians of Canada, the Wards of the Nation, Our Allies in the Revolutionary War, Our Brothers- in-Arms in the Great War. He charges that, for 1894-1908, within five years of entry 30% to 60% of students had died, an avoidable mortality rate had healthy children not been exposed to children with tuberculosis: A "trail of disease and death has gone on almost unchecked by any serious efforts on the part of the Department of Indian Affairs." His 1907 recommendations on tuberculosis control not given effect, he says, "owing to the active opposition of Mr. D.C. Scott."

- 1923 – "Residential Schools" adopted as official term, replacing "boarding" (55) and "industrial" (16), housing 5,347 children.

- 1932 – Scott retires as Deputy Superintendent General after more than 52 years in the department. The anthologist John Garvin writes that Scott's "policy of assimilating the Indians had been so much in keeping with the thinking of the time that he was widely praised for his capable administration." He embodied a fundamental contradiction: While a rigid and often heartless bureaucrat, "his sensibilities as a poet [were] saddened by the waning of an ancient culture" (Canadian Encyclopedia).

- 1939 – 9,027 children are in 79 residential schools run by Catholic (60%), Anglican (25%), United and Presbyterian churches. "1939 [was] the approximate mid-point of the history of the system": John S. Milloy, A National Crime.

- 1944 – Consensus develops among senior Indian Affairs officials that integration into provincial systems should replace segregated Aboriginal education.
- 1951 – Indian Act of 1876, with many amendments, repealed; replaced with modernized Indian Act (today's Act, with amendments) conceptually similar to previous Act.

- 1955 – Jean Lesage, Minister of Northern Affairs and National Resources, department responsible for Inuit (then known as Eskimos), gets Cabinet approval for broad education policy in North. General policy is to substitute settlements for nomadic life. A school is built at Chesterfield Inlet, followed by Coppermine, and ten "hostels." Some Inuit had formerly been sent south to Indian Affairs schools. "Destitute" Métis were sometimes also enrolled.

- 1969 – Indian Affairs takes over sole management of residential schools from churches.

- 1969 – Indian Affairs Minister Jean Chretien produces assimilationist "White Paper" to abolish Indian status; strongly opposed by Indian organizations. Alberta Indian Association produces Citizens Plus, known as "Red Paper," in response. White Paper retracted two years later.

- 1971 – Blue Quills School, St. Paul, AB, becomes first Indian-run school, following month-long contentious occupation by elders and others.
- 1972 – National Indian Brotherhood (predecessor of Assembly of First Nations) produces Indian Control of Indian Education, advocating greater band control of education on reserves; adopted next year by government.

- 1975 – Six residential schools close this year; 15 remain.
- 1976 – NIB proposes amendments to Indian Act to provide legal basis for Indian control of education; rejected by government.

- 1978 – National Film Board produces first film ever on residential schools: Wandering Spirit Survival School, about a non-traditional school organized by parents who had themselves survived residential schools.
- 1984 – 187 bands are operating own (day) schools, half in B.C.; the rest mainly on Prairies.

- 1993 – Archbishop Michael Peers, Primate of Anglican Church of Canada, apologizes to survivors of Indian residential schools on behalf of the Church.
- 1996 – Gordon Indian Residential School, Punnichy, Saskatchewan, closes; last of 139 Indian Residential Schools in Canada.

The Report of the Royal Commission on Aboriginal Peoples recommends public investigation into violence and abuses at residential schools. Report brings these issues to national attention.
- 1998 – Minister of Indian Affairs Jane Stewart responds with "Statement of Reconciliation," acknowledging government's role, stating "sexual and physical abuse ... should never have happened. To those of you who suffered this tragedy at residential schools, we are deeply sorry." Established Aboriginal Healing Foundation to assist Aboriginal communities to build healing processes, with $350 million endowment. Express apology had to wait until 2008.

- 2001 – Federal Office of Indian Residential Schools Resolution Canada created to manage and resolve large number of abuse claims filed by former students, resulting in 17 court judgments.

- 2003 – National Resolution Framework launched, including Alternative Dispute Resolution process, an out of court process providing compensation and psychological support for former students who were physically or sexually abused or had been wrongfully confined.

- 2004 – Assembly of First Nations (AFN) Report on Canada's Dispute Resolution Plan tocompensate for Abuses in Indian Residential Schools leads to resolution discussions. RCMP Commissioner Giuliano Zaccardelli expresses sorrow for the force's role in the residential school system.

- 2005 – $1.9 billion compensation package announced to benefit former residential school students.

- 2007 – Indian Residential Schools Settlement Agreement, largest class action settlement in Canadian history, negotiated and approved by parties, and Courts in nine jurisdictions, implemented. Of the 139 schools ultimately included in the settlement, 64 were Roman Catholic, 35 Anglican, 14 United Church, and the balance other or no denomination. The objective was reconciliation with the estimated 80,000 former students then still living, of over 150,000 enrolled since 1879. Elements are,
  - Common Experience Payment to be paid to all eligible former students who resided at a recognized Indian Residential School;
  - Independent Assessment Process for claims of sexual or serious physical abuse;
  - Establishment of a Truth and Reconciliation Commission;
    - •Commemoration Activities;

- •Measures to support healing such as the Indian Residential Schools Resolution Health Support Program and an endowment to the Aboriginal Healing Foundation.

Survivors report harsh and cruel punishments, suicides of others, physical, psychological and sexual abuse, poor quality and meagre rations and shabby clothing in the schools, and inability on leaving to belong in either the Aboriginal or larger world. Posttraumatic stress disorder, major depression, anxiety disorder and borderline personality disorder have been diagnosed, and many have criminal records.

- 2008 – Prime Minister Harper offers formal apology in Parliament for the Indian Residential Schools, in presence of Aboriginal delegates and church leaders. Indian Residential Schools Truth and Reconciliation Commission established June 1, with five-year mandate, later extended to 2015.

- 2009 – AFN Chief Phil Fontaine meets Pope Benedict XVI at Vatican. Pope Benedict expresses "sorrow" and "sympathy and prayerful solidarity," but avoids apologizing.

After a rocky start, with resignations of original Commissioners, Truth and Reconciliation Commission begins work under Justice Murray Sinclair, an Aboriginal Manitoba judge who became the province's Associate Chief Justice in 1988.

- 2010 – Truth and Reconciliation Commission begins hearings in Winnipeg.

- 2011 – University of Manitoba president David Barnard apologizes to Truth and Reconciliation Commission of Canada for institution's role in educating people who operated the residential school system.

- 2012 – Truth and Reconciliation Commission releases Interim Report. Reviews progress, explains statement gathering and document collection process. Tells of degrading treatment, unwarranted punishments, and physical and sexual abuse by "loveless institutions." Makes numerous recommendations respecting public education about residential schools and about mental health and wellness programs, especially in the North, and that Canada and churches establish a cultural revival fund.
Notes mandate to establish a National Research Centre.
Over 105,000 applications for Common Experience Payments were received by Canada by September 19, 2012, deadline; over 79,000 were found eligible and paid, the average amount being $19, 412.

- 2014 – Commission hearings in more than 300 communities wrap up. "National Events," in Winnipeg, Inuvik, Halifax, Saskatoon, Montreal and Vancouver were held, as required by the Settlement Agreement, the final one taking place March 27-30 in Edmonton.

- 2015 – Final year for the Truth and Reconciliation Commission; related events occur:
August 16: Dr. Peter Bryce (1853-1932), author of The Story of a National Crime, is honoured by the unveiling of a plaque in his honour at Ottawa's Beechwood Cemetery, the National Cemetery of Canada.
November 1: The plaque at Beechwood Cemetery honouring Scott as a poet modified to include mention of his role in residential schools.
December 15: The massive final six-volume, 3,231-page TRC report is released. The TRC also produced a summary and five other companion volumes, 2012-15.
December 18: The Truth and Reconciliation Commission

closes its doors. As required by the Settlement Agreement, the National Centre for Truth and Reconciliation opens, with a mandate to hold and make accessible all of the materials gathered by the Commission throughout its mandate. It is located at 177 Dysart Road on the University of Manitoba Fort Garry Campus in south Winnipeg: nctr.ca.

The Report looks to the future: "Reconciliation is not about 'closing a sad chapter in Canada's past,' but about opening new healing pathways of reconciliation that are forged in truth and justice."

Assimilation policy was cultural genocide, "the destruction of those structures and practices that allow [a targeted] group to continue as a group."

At the heart of the Report are 94 "Calls to Action," under two main headings, "Legacy" and "Reconciliation." Governments, educational, professional and sports bodies, media, churches (including the Pope), the arts, and the corporate sector are called to action. "Legacy" calls are to "redress the legacy of residential schools" in the areas of child welfare, education, language and culture, health, and justice. Under "Justice," an "Investigation into missing and murdered Aboriginal women and girls" is called for, and is underway. "Reconciliation" calls are more general, the most numerous calling for "full" adoption and implementation of the United Nations Declaration of the Rights of Indigenous Peoples "as the framework for reconciliation," and related matters. This is controversial, and the federal government is equivocal. Other calls are for a "Covenant of Reconciliation," a National Council for Reconciliation, church apologies, and a National Day for Truth and Reconciliation as a statutory holiday. Many non-governmental entities, including law societies, have acted in response to the Report.

- 2016 – The Supreme Court of Newfoundland and Labrador approves a $50 million settlement of five class action lawsuits on behalf of indigenous former students from Labrador who attended one of the residential schools at Cartwright (Lockwood), North West River (Yale), Makkovik and Nain (in Labrador) and St. Anthony (on the island of Newfoundland). The schools were established by the International Grenfell Association or by the Moravian Mission well before 1949 when Newfoundland joined Canada, but subsequently received government support until the last one closed in 1980.

- 2017 – Prime Minister Trudeau apologizes, at Happy Valley-Goose Bay, NL, to the indigenous former students who attended residential schools in Newfoundland and Labrador, and to their "families, loved ones and communities impacted by these schools for the painful and sometimes tragic legacy these schools left behind." Residential school students were not included in Prime Minister Harper's 2008 apology, having been excluded from the 2007 Indian Residential Schools Settlement Agreement in the province.

7

The International Tribunal for the Disappeared

The International Tribunal for the Disappeared of Canada offer a more expanded and somewhat darker timeline, which unfortunately is probably closer to historical accuracy in the opinion of the author. The following timeline is reprinted with permission and appears in Kevin Annett's book, Murder by Decree, which can be downloaded for free at https://.murderbydecree.com.

- 1840 - The Act of Union creates a single nation of the former French and English-speaking enclaves of Lower and Upper Canada. The Act establishes what will become Canada on an explicitly "assimilationist" basis dominated by the English and committed to eliminating all distinctive cultures, whether French speaking or aboriginal.
- 1850 - Indigenous nations in eastern Canada have been decimated by deliberately introduced diseases to barely ten percent of their pre-contact numbers. Local Indian schools run by the Church of England, like the Mohawk school in Brantford, ON, experience enormous death rates of over 40%. Tribes west of the Lake Head remain untouched by this plague, except on the west coast where Europeans are beginning to settle.
- 1857 - The Gradual Civilization Act is passed in the Canadian legislature, legally eradicating all indigenous people who do

not "enfranchise" and surrender their land titles and nationhood.
- 1859 - Roman Catholic missions are established throughout what will become British Columbia under Jesuit direction. Bishop Paul Durieu creates a model to exterminate traditional Indian leaders and culture and replace them with church-controlled puppet leaders: a model that will serve as the basis for the later Indian residential school system.
- 1862 - Major smallpox epidemics are deliberately introduced among Chilcotin, Cowichan and other west coast tribes by Church of England missionaries like John Sheepshanks. Over 90% of the Indians inoculated by Sheepshanks and others will die within weeks, and land speculators like Sheepshanks' fellow investors in the Hudson's Bay Company will then occupy the land emptied of Indians.
- 1869-70 - The first failed uprising of the mixed-blood Metis people near Winnipeg prompts the Canadian government to proclaim its sovereignty "from sea to sea" and commence the building of a national railway, along with massive European immigration onto western Indian lands.
- 1870 - The British Crown through the Canadian Parliament establishes a "clergy reserve" system granting huge swaths of stolen indigenous land to any Anglican or Catholic missionary who settles on such land, usually near to the advancing Canadian Pacific Railway (CPR).
- 1873 - The Royal Northwest Mounted Police, forerunner of the RCMP, is established as a para-military force with absolute jurisdiction across Canada. Its mandate includes forcibly removing all Indians from within fifty miles of the CPR and incarcerating them on impoverished "reservations".
- 1876 - CPR lawyer and Prime Minister John A. MacDonald proclaims through Order in Council the Indian Act, which reduces all Indians and Metis people to the status of non-citizens

THE INTERNATIONAL TRIBUNAL FOR THE DISAPPEARED - | 49 |

and "legal wards of the state in perpetuity". Henceforth, no Indian can vote, sue in court, own land, or enjoy any civil or legal rights. This "legal ward" status of all reservation Indians continues to the present day in Canada.

- 1886 - Following the crushing of the Second Metis Rebellion the CPR is completed, linking the west and east coasts. The same year, all west coast aboriginal ceremonies like the Potlatch are outlawed and hundreds of traditional native leaders are murdered or jailed.
- 1889 - The Indian residential school system is launched along with the federal Department of Indian Affairs (DIA), which sponsors the "schools" in partnership with the Roman Catholic, Anglican, Methodist, and Presbyterian churches (the latter two will form the United Church of Canada in 1925.) In Alberta, the death rate in such "schools" exceeds 40% in the very first year they open, compared to a mortality of barely 5% on the reservations from which the children are taken.
- 1891 - The first official report that documents massive deaths in the residential schools is issued to the DIA by Dr. George Orton, who claims that the cause is rampant tuberculosis among children that is being "encouraged by school staff". Orton's report is ignored by the DIA.
- 1903 - The flood of reports of an enormous death rate in the western residential schools provokes the DIA to cease publishing "total spectrum" death reports among children, meaning that many such deaths will now be officially censored by the government.
- 1905 - Indians in western Canada has been depopulated to less than 5% of their original number. Over 100 residential schools are in operation, two thirds of them run by the Roman Catholics.
- 1907 - DIA medical officer Dr. Peter Bryce conducts a tour of all western residential schools and issues a damning report

that claims, "conditions are being deliberately created to spread infectious disease." Bryce documents that an average 40% to 60% of school children are dying because of a "routine practice" of housing the sick with the healthy and denying them all medical treatment. He claims that the staff is deliberately hiding the evidence of this genocidal practice.

- November 15, 1907 - The Ottawa Citizen and Montreal Gazette newspapers quote Dr. Bryce's report under the headline "Schools aid white plague – Startling Death Rolls Revealed". Despite this, Bryce is silenced by DIA Deputy Superintendent Duncan Campbell Scott and his report is ignored.

- November 1909 - After conducting further investigations that confirm the murderous practices by residential school staff, Dr. Peter Bryce calls for the churches to be removed from operating the residential schools. Bryce is then fired from his position by Scott and banned from the civil service, although in 1920 he will publish his account in his book A National Crime.

- November 1910 - Despite Bryce's findings, Duncan Campbell Scott of the DIA institutionalizes church control over the schools through a joint contract with the Catholic and Protestant churches. This contract provides government funding and "protection" for the schools, including the use of the RCMP to incarcerate and hunt down Indian children. In return, the churches have complete day to day control of the schools and hire and fire their Principals and staff.

- 1910 - Later government records reveal that during the first decade of the 20th century, the net population of Indians in Canada declined by over 20%, an unprecedented level "not explained by any demographic or environmental factors." The use of residential schools as a breeding ground for infectious disease that is then disseminated through native communities is one factor in this depopulation.

- February 1919 - Despite the continuing high death rates and murderous conditions in the residential schools, Duncan Campbell Scott abolishes all medical inspection in them and prohibits further studies of health conditions in the schools. Within a year, the death rates in western native communities will nearly triple. (Figure 5) This mortality is also caused by a routine practice of sending sick children home to infect their families with smallpox and tuberculosis.
- June 8, 1920 - Prime Minister Arthur Meighen states in Parliament that no provision for the health of Indians was ever included in the federal Health Act or Department. "It was purposely left out of the Act."
- July 1, 1920 - Incarceration in the residential schools is made mandatory under a federal law passed through Order in Council. Every Indian child seven years and older must attend a school or its parents will go to jail.
- July 19, 1924 - A state church is created by an Act of Parliament – the United Church of Canada – to "Canadianize and Christianize the foreign born and the heathens." This foundational genocidal purpose is affirmed not only through the church's operation of residential schools and Indian hospitals where Indian children die en masse, but in their foundational policy statements concerning their aim to "dispossess" aboriginals of their traditions.
- May 1925 - Provincial laws in British Columbia and Alberta – where most "unassimilated" Indians are concentrated – strips aboriginal people of the right to consult or hire a lawyer, or even represent themselves in a court of law. Neither is any lawyer allowed to take on an aboriginal client.
- 1929-1933 - Sexual Sterilization laws are passed in both provinces' legislatures, allowing any inmate of an Indian residential school to be involuntarily sterilized at the decision of the

school Principal, a church employee. Thousands of children and adults are sexually neutered by these laws.

- 1929-1933 - The Canadian government relinquishes its traditional legal guardianship over Indian children and grants such power to the residential school Principal, a church employee.
- February 1934 - An attempt by the government to abolish residential schools is thwarted because of massive pressure and threats brought by all the churches running the schools.
- October 1935 - A genocidal "two standards of health care" system in residential schools is confirmed by Dr. C. Pitts in a letter that states "... were I to apply the standards of health to them (Indians) that is applied to children of the white schools, that (sic) I should have to discharge 90% of them and there would be no school left." Pitts is referring to the Lejac Catholic School in northern British Columbia, and admits that a lower standard of health care is applied to them.
- 1937-38 - School records confirm that children infected with tuberculosis are admitted to west coast Indian schools, and officials refer to the fact that the Indian Affairs department "will not hospitalize Indians suffering from pulmonary tuberculosis."
- January 1939 - Cowichan Indian children are widely used in medical experiments conducted by "German speaking doctors" at the Catholic Kuper Island School in British Columbia. Many of them die, according to two survivors, but the RCMP suppresses inquiries by local police.
- 1940-45 - Under the cover of war, involuntary experimental research is commenced on many residential school children by the Defense Research Board (DRB) in Ottawa. The research includes drug testing, deliberate starvation, behavior modification, pain threshold studies, chemical weapons testing and sterilizing methods. These tests are conducted in the schools, at military bases, and at special laboratories and Indian hospitals

THE INTERNATIONAL TRIBUNAL FOR THE DISAPPEARED — | 53 |

run jointly with the United, Anglican and Catholic churches, and will continue for decades.

- 1946-8 - Hundreds of Nazi SS doctors and researchers are granted citizenship in Canada under the joint British American "Project Paperclip", and work under cover identities and military supervision in the aforementioned experimental programs.

- 1947 - Canadian U.N. diplomat and future Prime Minister Lester Pearson helps to redefine genocide in the proposed United Nations Convention in order to make it inapplicable to Canadian Indian residential schools. Enabling legislation to allow its application in Canada is blocked in Parliament.

- 1958 - The government again attempts to close residential schools and meets hostile resistance and threats of political action by all three churches operating the schools. The plan is dropped.

- 1960 - Revisions to the Revised Statues of British Columbia legally define an aboriginal as "an uncivilized person, destitute of the knowledge of God and of any fixed and clear belief in religion or in a future state of rewards and punishments."

- 1962 - A government plan later entitled the "Sixties Scoop" covertly begins to privatize residential schools by transferring huge numbers of Indian children into non-aboriginal homes through state subsidized foster agencies. Thousands of children have their identity and family life destroyed in this manner without setting foot in a residential school.

- 1965 - Government document destruction teams obliterate countless residential school records related to the identity and deaths of students, in anticipation of the phasing out of the schools.

- 1969 - Indian Affairs minister and future Prime Minister Jean Chretien affirms an "assimilationist" policy of legally exterminating native nations in a federal "White Paper" introduced in Parliament.

- 1970 - Native protests against the White Paper, including the seizure and occupation of Bluequills residential school in Alberta by aboriginal parents, forces the government to begin the process of turning over residential schools to the control of local tribal councils.
- 1972 - The government destroys thousands of Indian Affairs records including personnel files with information on residential school history and aboriginal land deeds, making the verification of school crimes and native land claims impossible.
- 1975 - A majority of residential schools formerly run by the churches are now either closed or under the management of local Indian band councils. Nevertheless, many of the same crimes and tortures against children continue, often at the hands of aboriginal staff members.
- 1982 - The Government funds and establishes the puppet aboriginal organization known as the "Assembly of First Nations" (AFN), consisting of 600 self-appointed state funded tribal "chiefs". The AFN claims to "represent" all aboriginals in Canada, but it refuses all calls for indigenous sovereignty or to investigate the residential schools genocide.
- October 1989 - Nora Bernard, an east coast native survivor of the Shubenacadie Catholic residential school, commences the first lawsuit against both the church and the government for harm she suffered. Nora refers to "our genocide". She will be murdered in December, 2007 just prior to the launching of the government cover up known as the "Truth and Reconciliation Commission" (TRC).
- October 1990 - AFN head and government employee "Chief" Phil Fontaine, in response to the Nora Bernard residential school lawsuit, speaks publicly of "abuses" in the schools and establishes a benign, AFN monopoly over the issue that never mentions the death of children or genocide.

- March 1994 - In Port Alberni, the killing of children in the local United Church residential school is addressed by Rev. Kevin Annett and native survivors from his pulpit. Annett is told by church officers to refrain from addressing the issue and is threatened with firing.
- January 23, 1995 - Kevin Annett is fired without cause after reporting more stories of residential school killings and of the theft of west coast native land by his United Church employer and its business partner the logging company MacMillan-Bloedel. His unusual firing is addressed by a Vancouver Sun columnist that summer, as MacMillan-Bloedel issues a payoff to the United Church in Port Alberni.
- December 13, 1995 - The first account of the murder of a residential school child, Maisie Shaw, is made by eyewitness Harriett Nahanee at a rally held by fired United Church minister Kevin Annett, and is reported by the Vancouver Sun newspaper. A week later, a second such murder, of a boy named Albert Gray, is reported by eyewitness Archie Frank, and is again reported by the Sun. Beaten to death for theft of a prune, by Mark Hume, Vancouver Sun, December 20, 1995 Both eyewitnesses claim the killer was Principal Alfred Caldwell. The RCMP refuses to investigate.
- February 1, 1996 - The first class action lawsuit by residential school survivors in Canada opens in the British Columbia Supreme Court, brought by fifteen former students at the Alberni School against the United Church and government. Kevin Annett is an adviser to the plaintiffs.
- February 3, 1996 - The United Church begins closed, internal disciplinary proceedings against Kevin Annett to permanently expel him from the ministry, which will occur the next year at a cost to the church of over $250,000. Annett will never be charged by the church with any wrongdoing.

- 1997-1998 - Other Canadian newspapers begin to report eyewitness allegations of killings in residential schools, including those gathered in healing circles convened by Kevin Annett and Harriet Nahanee.
- February 9, 1998 - At a public rally of over 600 people in Vancouver, many of them aboriginal, the Truth Commission into Genocide in Canada (TCGC) is established as an independent, open inquiry into residential school crimes. Kevin Annett is elected as its General Secretary.
- June 6, 1998 - Justice Donald Brenner of the British Columbia Supreme Court rules that the United Church and government of Canada are equally liable for damages to inmates in residential schools, opening the door to thousands of subsequent lawsuits by survivors against all three churches.
- June 12-14, 1998 - The first independent inquiry into residential school crimes is convened in Vancouver by the United Nations affiliate International Human Rights Association of American Minorities (IHRAAM), upon the invitation of TCGC leaders Harriett Nahanee and Kevin Annett. The inquiry hears from twenty-eight eyewitnesses to these crimes and concludes that "every act defined as genocide under international law occurred in Canadian Indian residential schools". None of the church and government officials subpoenaed by IHRAAM respond to or refute this claim. IHRAAM recommends to United Nations High Commissioner Mary Robinson that an international tribunal be held into these crimes, but Robinson never replies.
- June 20, 1998 - The Globe and Mail is the only media in Canada to report the IHRAAM hearings.
- October 27, 1998 - The Province newspaper reports an admission by United Church lawyers that the church has engaged in a cover up of residential school crimes with the government

since at least 1960, and that church officials kidnapped child to bring them into the schools.
- January 1999 - The residential school crimes and the IHRAAM - TCGC inquiry are reported on for the first time outside of Canada, in the British magazine The New Internationalist. But the publication is pressured by Crown lawyers to desist from any subsequent coverage of the issue.
- March 1999 - In response to the IHRAAM inquiry and escalating lawsuits, the Canadian government creates an "Aboriginal Healing Fund" (AHF) that is used as a hush fund for survivors. Any of the AHF recipients must first agree never to sue the government or churches that ran the schools.
- April 26, 2000 - In the first of many "spin doctoring" of residential school atrocities, Health Canada admits that it conducted "limited" experiments on school children during the 1950's by denying them dental care, food, and vitamins, but provides no details.
- 2000-2001 - Facing over ten thousand individual lawsuits by school survivors, the government under church pressure legislates a limit on the scope of such lawsuits and assumes primary financial liability for residential school damages, ignoring the Brenner joint-liability legal decision of 1998. Crown courts in Alberta and Ontario impose similar restrictions and deny survivors the right to sue the church and state for genocide.
- February 1, 2001 - The TCGC publishes the first documentation of deliberate genocide in Canadian residential schools, "Hidden from History: The Canadian Holocaust" by Kevin Annett. Over 1,000 copies are sent to the media, politicians, and many residential school survivors.
- August 14, 2001 - The British Columbia Court of Appeals, under government pressure, reverses the 1998 Brenner Decision and places the entire financial liability for residential

school damages on the federal government and taxpayer, absolving the churches of any financial liability.
- 2001-2004 - The TCGC mounts a broad public education campaign about the residential schools' genocide, picketing the churches responsible and holding public forums across Canada at which survivors tell their stories and name names. The Commission begins its own radio program on Vancouver Co-op Radio, Hidden from History, hosted by Kevin Annett. The program will air for nine years until it is terminated from government pressure.
- December 29, 2004 - After being contacted by Kevin Annett, a federation of Mayan indigenous groups issues a Denuncia or official demand to the Canadian government to disclose its evidence of the genocide of native people in Canada. Receiving no reply, the Mayans take their Denuncia of the Canadian Genocide to the United Nations.
- April 15, 2005 - The TCGC and its affiliate The Friends and Relatives of the Disappeared (FRD) hold the first Aboriginal Holocaust Remembrance Day in Vancouver outside Catholic, Anglican, and United churches. For the first time speakers issue a call for the repatriation of the remains of children who died at the residential schools. The event is widely reported in the media.
- March-October 2006 - Numerous accounts of mass graves of children at or near former Indian residential schools are received by the TCGC and FRD, prompting the production of the first documentary film on genocide in Canada: Unrepentant.
- January – May 2007 - Unrepentant is released worldwide to hundreds of thousands of viewers and wins Best Documentary at the Los Angeles Independent Film Festival. FRD and Kevin Annett commence high profile occupations of Catholic, Anglican and United churches in Vancouver Winnipeg and Toronto, which are widely reported in the media. A report sur-

faces that residential school documents were deliberately destroyed by the government.

- April 2007 - After seeing Unrepentant, Member of Parliament Gary Merasty calls on the government to begin repatriating the remains of residential school children. Indian Affairs minister Jim Prentice announces a Missing Children's Task Force that never convenes. But Prentice also hints at the formation of a Truth and Reconciliation Commission to investigate residential school deaths.
- April 24, 2007 The Globe and Mail newspaper publishes a front page article confirming the 50% death rate in residential schools.
- April 10, 2008 - Kevin Annett and FRD release to the world media a list of twenty-eight mass grave sites at or near former Indian residential schools across Canada. Neither Annett nor any FRD member is ever contacted by the police or government about the grave sites.
- April 15, 2008 - On the FRD's fourth Aboriginal Holocaust Memorial Day, the government issues a statement that although "enormous numbers of deaths" occurred in residential schools, no criminal charges will be laid against the churches that ran the schools, thereby legally indemnifying them from any prosecution. The churches then all quickly endorse the proposed Truth and Reconciliation Commission.
- June 1, 2008 - The Truth and Reconciliation Commission (TRC) is launched by the government after its officers are nominated by the three churches and approved by the Prime Minister's office. Its restricted mandate forbids it from laying criminal charges, issuing subpoenas, investigating homicides, or taking down as evidence the names of any residential school perpetrators. And over half of all school survivors are disqualified from any compensation by the government.

- June 11, 2008 - Prime Minister Stephen Harper issues a formal apology in Parliament for Indian residential schools, not mentioning the deaths of students or the involvement of churches in the schools. But Bloc Quebecois leader Gilles Duceppe refers to the "mass graves" of Indian children.
- December 14, 2009 - FRD organizer and residential school survivor Bingo Dawson, is beaten to death by three Vancouver policemen, according to eyewitness Ricky Lavallee. The cause of death is listed as "alcohol poisoning" although an accompanying toxicology report states that no alcohol or drugs were found in his bloodstream. Bingo is the first of six FRD members who will die of foul play between 2009 and 2012.
- June 15, 2010 - The International Tribunal into Crimes of Church and State (ITCCS) is established in Dublin by six organizations and survivors of church tortures. Its mandate is to prosecute both church and state for crimes committed against children and disestablish such unlawful authorities. The Canadian government's TRC issues a statement the same week that its research has uncovered evidence of the graves of children at residential school sites but gives no details.
- August 2010 - The film Unrepentant is broadcast in four languages to over ten million viewers on Swiss and German television. Kevin Annett's new book Unrepentant: Disrobing the Emperor is published in London. But on August 9, Kevin's long standing radio program Hidden from History is canceled without cause or explanation by Vancouver Co-op radio, which is government funded.
- April 10, 2011 - Ten Mohawk elders invite Kevin Annett to their territory at Brantford, Ontario to assist them in recovering the remains of children in mass graves next to the oldest residential school in Canada, the Mohawk Institute, and run by the Church of England. The next month, on May 29, while doing

archival research in London, Kevin is deported from England without cause.

- October-December 2011 - The ITCCS and Mohawk elders begin their joint investigation into the missing children at the Brantford school by employing grand penetrating radar. Suspected grave sites are located almost immediately based on surviving eyewitness account. Actual excavation of such a site commences in November and uncovers buttons of school uniforms and sixteen bone samples, one of which is confirmed by forensic experts to be from a small child. This first recovery of bones from a residential school grave goes completely unreported in the Canadian media, despite a Mohawk press conference in November.
- June 3, 2015 - Canada acknowledges that genocide occurred within the Indian residential school system and that thousands of children died as a result. (New York Times, 3/6/2015)
- March 1, 2016 - Counter Report to the TRC's misinformation is issued by the International Tribunal for the Disappeared of Canada (ITDC) and Kevin Annett.

This timeline is extensively sourced with extensive documentation for almost every point and the reader is encouraged to check out http://murderbydecree.com/ and the recent discovery of thousands of unmarked graves across Canada lends yet more support for these claims.

[illegible] arrived in London, Kevin is [illegible] from England without cause.

- October–December 2014: The UCC [illegible] [illegible] investigation [illegible] the [illegible] by employing grand [illegible] [illegible] immediately [illegible] giving [illegible] and [illegible] and [illegible] [illegible] [illegible] [illegible] [illegible] experts [illegible] [illegible] [illegible] [illegible] in [illegible] despite [illegible] in November.
- [illegible] 2015: Canada [illegible] [illegible] system and that [illegible] (2015).
- March [illegible] 2015: [illegible] the International Tribunal for the Disappeared of Canada (ITDC) and [illegible].

The [illegible] [illegible] in [illegible] [illegible] and the [illegible] Canada [illegible].

The Ugly

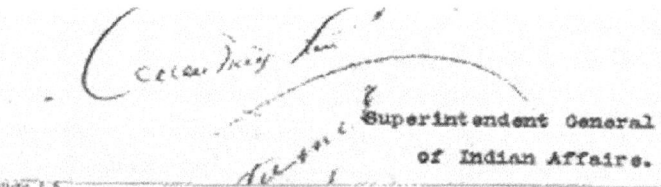

Figure 1.5

TB rate: Aboriginal and total population, British Columbia, 1918-29

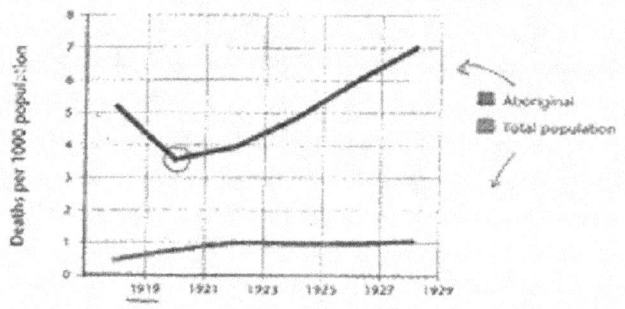

Source: British Columbia, Vital Statistics, 'Reports,' 1918-36, *Sessional Papers*, 1919-1932.

8

Tuberculosis

Reprinted with permission from The Truth Commission into Genocide in Canada.
From Hidden from History: The Canadian Holocaust.

In 1909, Dr. Peter Bryce of the Ontario Health Department was hired by the Indian Affairs Department in Ottawa to tour the Indian residential schools in western Canada and British Columbia and report on the health conditions there. Bryce's report so scandalized the government and the churches that it was officially buried, and only surfaced in 1922 when Bryce—who was forced out of the civil service for the honesty of his report—wrote a book about it entitled The Story of a National Crime: Being a Record of the Health Conditions of the Indians of Canada from 1904 to 1921. (Bryce, 1922).

In his report, Dr. Bryce claimed that Indian children were being systematically and deliberately killed in the residential schools. He cited an average mortality rate of between 35% and 60% and alleged that staff and church officials were regularly withholding or falsifying records and other evidence of children's deaths. Further, Dr. Bryce claimed that a primary means of killing native children was to deliberately expose them to communicable diseases such as tuberculosis, and then deny them any medical care or treatment, a practice referred to by top Anglican Church leaders in The Globe and Mail on May 29,1953. In the words of Dr. Bryce,

"I believe the conditions are being deliberately created in our residential schools to spread infectious diseases... It is not unusual for children who are dying from consumption to be admitted to schools and housed alongside healthy children. This is a national crime."

In March 1998, two native eyewitnesses who attended west coast residential schools, William and Mabel Sport of Nanaimo, BC, confirmed Dr. Bryce's allegation. Both claim to have been deliberately exposed to tuberculosis by staff at both a Catholic and a United Church residential school during the 1940's

"I was forced to sleep in the same bed with kids who were dying of tuberculosis. That was at the Catholic Christie residential school around 1942. They were trying to kill us off, and it nearly worked. They did the same thing at Protestant Indian schools, three kids to a bed, healthy ones with the dying."
(Testimony of Mabel Sport to IHRAAM officers, Port Alberni, BC, March 31, 1998)

"Reverend Pitts, the Alberni school Principal, he forced me and eight other boys to eat this special food out of a different sort of can. It tasted really strange. And then all of us came down with tuberculosis. I was the only one to survive, 'cause my Dad broke into the school one night and got me out of there. All of the rest died from tuberculosis and they were never treated. Just left there to die. And their families were all told they had died of pneumonia. The plan was to kill us off in secret, you know. We all just began dying after eating that food. Two of my best friends were in that group that was poisoned. We were never allowed to speak of it, or go into the basement, where other murders happened. It was a death sentence to be sent to the Alberni school."
(Testimony of William Sport to IHRAAM officers, Port Alberni, BC, March 31, 1998)

Tribal elder George Harris of the Chemainus Nation on Vancouver Island confirms the Sports' story.

"We were expendable. Our lives had no value. Whenever we got sick at the Kuper Island school we were completely ignored. My mother was even forced to sleep in the same bed with kids who had tuberculosis. That was common. The church people were trying to kill us off. Tuberculosis spread like wildfire among us because of the policy of infecting us. So many of us died from that, and from the food they made us eat, which was rancid and filled with bugs. Anything was permitted if it killed Indians."

(Testimony of George Harris to the IHRAAM Tribunal, June 12, 1998)

This policy of deliberately infecting children with diseases under unhealthy conditions originated at the highest level of power in Canada; a fact attested to by the response of Indian Superintendent Duncan Scott to Dr. Bryce's report. Scott, the top Indian Affairs official in Canada at the time, wrote to his BC counterpart in 1910:

"It is readily acknowledged that Indian children lose their natural resistance to illness by habitating so closely in these schools, and that they die at a much higher rate than in their villages. But this alone does not justify a change in the policy of this Department, which is geared towards the final solution of our Indian Problem."

(DIA Superintendent D.C. Scott to BC Indian Agent-General Major D. McKay, April 12, 1910)

TUBERCULOSIS

363986

TABLE 1. - Summarizing the Results of Examinations in each School:-

Sarcee School.

Age				Father. Liv'g.	Mother. Liv'g.	Children.		Aver. chldn. liv'g.
5 or under.	8 to 9.	10 to 12.	14 to 18.			Liv.	Dead.	
5	5	3		13.	16.	45.	15.	3.6 25% d.r.

Temperature.				Pulse.		Respiration		Glands.		Nose.	
Nor'mal	98.4-99.1 to 99.	99.1-100 to 100.	100+ to 101.	Undr. 80.	81-91 to 80-120	17-21 to 20	21 to 25	25 plus	Nor'l.	Enlar.	Nor. Ab
2	5	7.	3.	4.	5. 7.	9.	7.	-	13.	5..	12. 4.

Throat.		Lungs.		Chest.		Gen. Appce.		Av. exp. chest.
Nor.	Abn.	Nor.	Abn.	Good.	Depd.	Fair	Poor	
15.	3.	3.	15.	5.	11.	10.	5.	3.1

* * * *

Blackfoot R. C. School.

Age				Father. Liv'g.	Mother. Liv'g.	Children.		Av. chldn. liv.
5 or under.	8 to 9.	10 to 12.	14 to 18.			Liv.	Dead.	
4.	13.	17.	5.	19.	25.	69.	29.	3'5 30% d.r.

Temperature.				Pulse.		Respiration.		Glands.		Chest.	
Nor.	98.4 to 99.	99.1 to 100.	100+ to 101.	Undr. 80.	81-91 to 80-120+	17-21 to 20.	21 to 25	25 plus	Nor. Abn.	Nor. Abn.	
-	21.	8.	5.	15.	11. 7.	13.	17.	5.	30. 5.	30. 5.	

Throat.		Lungs.		Chest.		Gen. Appce.		Av. Expn. Chest.
Nor.	Abn.	Nor.	Abn.	Good.	Dep'd.	Fair or Good.	Poor or Emaciated.	
25.	7.	2.	31.	18.	15.	15.	17.	2.8

* * * *

Peigan R. C. School.

40% death rate

Age				Father. Liv'g.	Mother. Liv'g.	Children.		Av. chldn. liv'g.
5 or under.	8 to 9.	10 to 12.	14 to 18.			Liv.	Dead.	
3.	11.	15.	2.	16.	15.	54.	37.	3.6

353988

Total Results of 243 pupils examined in 9 Indian Schools:_
(reading tables summarized)

Ages.				No. in family alive.				Aver.childn.liv'g.
5 or under.	6 - 9.	10 - 14.	15 - 18.	Father. Alive.	Mother. Alive.	Children. Alive.	Dead.	
9.	62.	99.	73.	145.	171.	537.	229.	3.7

Temperature.			Pulse.			Respiration.			Glands.		Nose.	
98.4 - 99.	99. - 100.	100. - 101.	Under 80.	81 - 90.	91 - 120.	17 - 20.	21 - 25.	25 & over.	Nor.	Abn.	Nor.	Abn.
93.	117.	23.	101.	70.	63.	97.	109.	29.	177.	58.	179.	54.

Throat.		Lungs.		Chest.		Av. exp'n of Chest.	Gen.Appce	
Nor.	Abnor.	Nor.	Abn.	Good.	Dep'd.		Fair or Good.	Poor or Emac'd
117.	116.	9.	226.	142.	91.	3.1 inches	160.	73.

9

The "Sixties Scoop"

Between 1951 and 1991, First Nation and Inuit children were taken into care and placed with non- Indigenous parents where they were not raised in accordance with their cultural traditions nor taught their traditional languages. In many cases they didn't even know they were Indigenous. This dark chapter in Canada's history is commonly referred to as the Sixties Scoop. Despite its name referencing the 1960s, the Sixties Scoop began in the mid-to-late 1950s and persisted into the 1980s. With an estimated 20,000 to upwards of 100,000 victims. Due to insufficient record keeping we may never know the actual numbers. What we do know for sure is that during this time programs like the Adopt Indian Metis (AIM) program, in which Indigenous children removed from traditional homes were presented like products or pets with pictures in newspapers and magazines throughout North America. These children, in many cases were to grow up with little to no knowledge of their indigenous roots and were often removed from siblings in the process. These children would never be told of their culture or have access to their Indian Status rights

A 1975 Government of Saskatchewan adoption services poster.

| 74 | - THE "SIXTIES SCOOP"

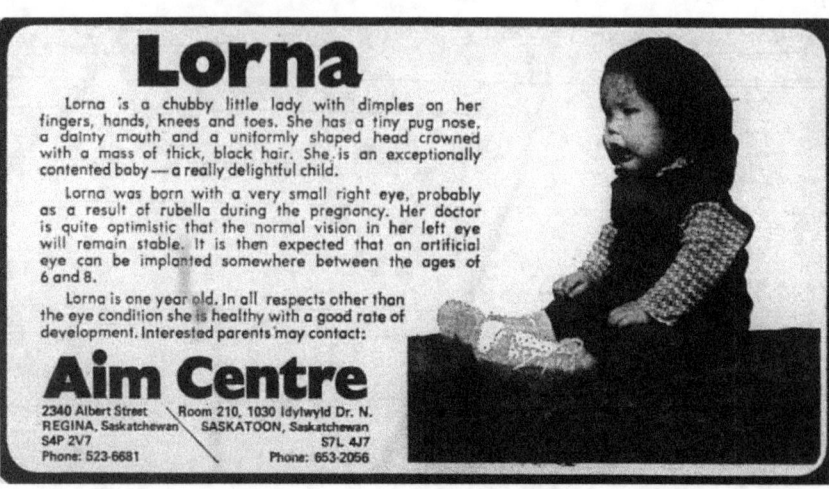

Regina Leader Post late 60's early 70's (exact date unknown)

THE "SIXTIES SCOOP"

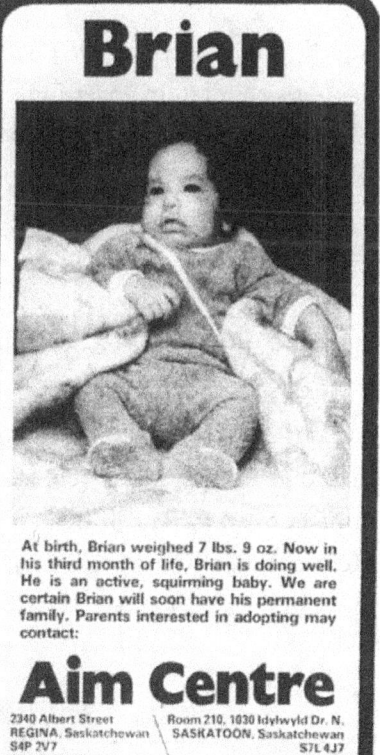

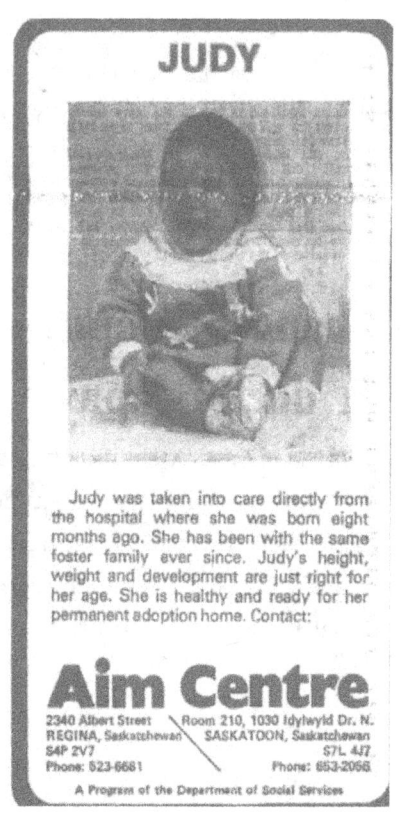

Regina Leader Post late 60's early 70's (exact date unknown)

| 76 | – THE "SIXTIES SCOOP"

Early Newspaper Ads for Adopt Indian and Métis, 1967 From Department of Social Services Collection, R-935, File I-49, Adopt Indian and Métis Program, SAB.

A.I.M. was launched by Saskatchewan Social Services in 1967 as a solution to the growing number of Indigenous children in government care. When Cyril Macdonald, Saskatchewan's minister of welfare, went on television that year to announce the program, he said

"The number of Indigenous children in care had been growing by 180 per year."

"While we have had reasonable success in placing white children for adoption, we have had great difficulty in placing Indian and Métis children."

He continues to state with optimism that the (AIM) program would "reduce the possibility of prejudice" that Indigenous children were facing, as well the cyclical nature of the indigenous kids and foster care homes. Because "After all, Indian and Métis children have the same potential as white. The only difference is the colour of their skin."

Saskatchewan Minister of Welfare goes on TV in 1967 to announce adoption program for Indigenous children

While the government policies that led to the Sixties Scoop were officially discontinued in the mid-1980s, a closer look at the child welfare documents and the Canadian Census data seems to indicate that in many ways the problem continues to persist to this day.

In December of 2018, The National Settlement between the Government of Canada and plaintiffs representing the group of Sixties Scoop Survivors who constitute "Eligible Class Members" was approved and a 750-million-dollar payout was announced. The agreement paves the way for each claimant to be eligible for between 25 and

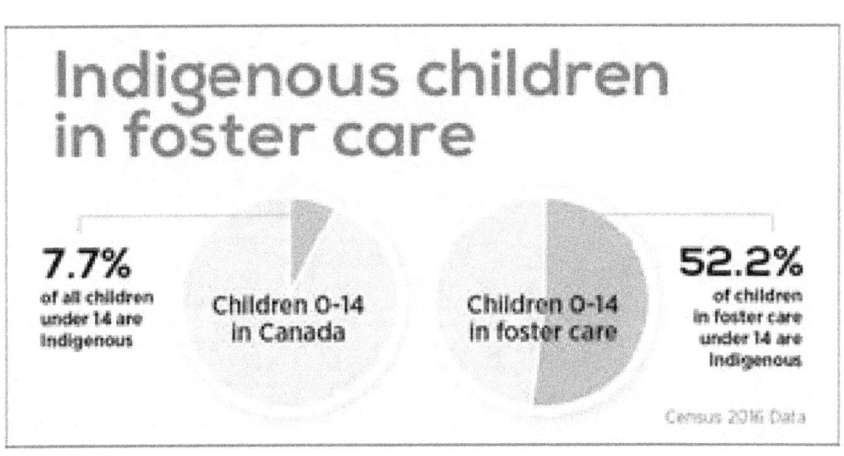

50 thousand dollars, up to a maximum of 750 million. At first glance this settlement may seem like a win, until we consider that "Eligible Class Member" does not include Metis or non-status Indians. Considering what we've learned about the number of Indigenous kids that have lost completely their access to family history, bloodlines, and status as a direct result of these policies. It's also worth mentioning that although special attention was paid to the fact the 75 million dollars in "legal fees" were awarded separate from the settlement amount of $750 million, the four law firms that represented the survivors (Wilson Christen LLP, Klein Lawyers, Koskie Minsky and the Merchant Law Group) stand to make 18.75 million PER firm, or 375 times the $50,000 maximum amount entertained per survivor. Although the fees were originally challenged, being called "excessive and unreasonable." The decision was overturned in 2021 and the fees will be paid by the federal government.

10

The Indigenous child removal system in Canada

An Examination of legal decision-making and Racial Bias
By Raven Sinclair - Professor, University of Regina (Saskatoon Campus), Saskatchewan, Canada from First People Child & Family Review.
Reprinted with permission.

The intense involvement of the child welfare system in Indigenous life emerged concurrently with the deterioration of Residential Schools in the 1950s. The transfer of responsibility for child welfare from federal to provincial control and the introduction of federal funding transfers through the Canada Assistance Plan in 1966 (Graham, Swift, & Delaney, 2008) allowed provinces to invest more resources into child welfare matters, leading to exponential growth in the Indigenous Child Welfare (Sinclair & Grekul, 2012).

By the 1970s, one in three First Nation children was separated from their families by adoption or fostering (Fournier & Crey, 1997), with Indigenous children making up 44% of all the children in care in Alberta, 51% in Saskatchewan, and 60% in Manitoba (McKenzie & Hudson, 1985, p.126). Currently, child in care statistics are even more alarming. Although Aboriginal children make up just 7% of the child population in Canada, they account for 48% of all foster children (Statistics Canada, 2013). Further, according to Turner, "three-quarters

(76%) of Aboriginal foster children lived in the four Western provinces... In Manitoba and Saskatchewan, 85% or more of foster children were Aboriginal children" (Turner, 2016). The high levels of children-in-care in the four western provinces skew the national data, which suggests that Indigenous children comprise 30-40% of children in care (Bennett et al., 2005). Gough, Trocmé,

Brown, Knoke and Blackstock (2005) observed that assimilation policies led to higher incidents of child removal and the overrepresentation of Indigenous children in care because Indigenous children were placed at twice the rate of non-Indigenous children, primarily due to socioeconomic conditions, alcohol abuse, neglect, criminal activity, and cognitive impairment.

The increase in children in care continues unabated with First Nations children spending over 60 million nights, or the equivalent of more than 180,000 years, in foster care between 1989 and 2012 (Blackstock, 2016). The exact numbers of Indigenous children placed in permanent alternative care during the 60s Scoop is not yet known, although research is currently underway (see Sinclair, 2016). In 1996, Indian Affairs (INAC) statistics (the A-list or Adoption List) tell us that 11,123 First Nations children (Canada, Erasmus, & Dussault, 1996, p. 48) were apprehended and subsequently adopted, primarily into non-Indigenous homes in Canada, the United States, and around the world between the years of 1960 and 1985 (Sinclair, 2007b). The list does not account for children who were not Status Indians according to the Indian Act, or who may have been status but were not recorded as such in the interests of promoting their "adoptability" by non-Indigenous families. "Métis" and "non-Status" Indigenous children may have been considered more socially desirable by potential adoptive parents (Sinclair, 2007b).

The intense increase in Indigenous child welfare apprehensions and relinquishments caused alarm in Indigenous communities and raised an outcry by Indigenous political leaders who argued that the removal of Indigenous children constituted genocide as per the Convention on the Prevention and Punishment of the Crime of Genocide, to which Canada is a signatory. The convention notes that genocide refers to "acts committed with intent to destroy, in whole or in part, a national, ethnical, racial or religious group" including item 2(e) which is "[f]orcibly transferring children of the group to another group" (UN General Assembly, 1948).

A public inquiry on the mass adoption of Indigenous children was conducted in Manitoba and a report was released in 1985. The report author, Justice Edwin Kimelman, condemned adoption practices in Manitoba, highlighting the fact that incomplete, inaccurate, and misleading information in child welfare files was the order of the day. The report stated, "...the Chairman [Kimelman] now states unequivocally that cultural genocide has been taking place in a systematic, routine manner" (Kimelman, 1985, p. 51). Kimelman's report led to an immediate moratorium on Indigenous adoption in Manitoba, which was followed, albeit informally, in other provinces. Ultimately his report altered adoption practices, and in Saskatchewan, for example, policies were developed that required the consent of families and First Nation band leadership to the adoption of Indigenous children.

At that time, "best interest of the child" evolved to include cultural considerations for Indigenous children. The "best interest of the child" is a legal construct used to guide child welfare decision-making. The "best interests of the child" criteria are set out by each province's legislation in assessing situations for Indigenous children in alternative care and for custody cases. Manitoba, for example, requires that consideration be given to the child's "cultural, linguistic, racial and religious heritage," (The Child and Family Services Act of 1985, 2013) while BC has a comprehensive list of "special Indigenous (Sinclair, 2016)

The Government of Canada's website currently acknowledges the problem and has this to say at the time of this writing:

Working in cooperation, partnership and mutual respect towards reform

- In January 2018, the federal government held a National Emergency Meeting with Indigenous peoples, representatives of Indigenous peoples and nations, the Assembly of First Nations, Inuit Tapiriit Kanatami and the Métis National Council, Indigenous service organizations, experts and practitioners, elders, grandmothers and youth with lived experience. At the meeting, the Government of Canada committed to Six Points of Action that include the potential for federal legislation, as called for in TRC Call to Action #4.
- A resolution passed in May of 2018 by the Assembly of First Nations supported the establishment of federal-enabling legislation for First Nations. An Interim Report by the National Advisory Committee on First Nations Child and Family Services also called for new federal legislation.
- During the summer and fall of 2018, the Government of Canada has been actively engaging with national, regional, and community organizations representatives of First Nations, Inuit and the Métis Nation, as well as Treaty Nations, self-governing First Nations, experts and those with lived experience. This engagement included activities with community leaders, representatives of the Assembly of First Nations, the Inuit Tapiriit Kanatami and the Métis Nation, Indigenous service organizations, provinces and territories, experts, child advocates, elders, youth and women. Over 65 Engagement Sessions have been held with nearly 2,000 participants. These sessions are part of the co-development for a legislative approach that sets the stage for comprehensive reform.

Indigenous peoples driving change

Some of the feedback given to the federal government during these extensive engagement sessions included the need to address principles, including those embodied in the United Nations Convention on the Rights of the Child (UNCRC), such as:

- In all actions concerning children, whether undertaken by public or private social welfare institutions, courts of law, administrative authorities or legislative bodies, the best interests of the child shall be the primary consideration. (UNCRC, Article 3)

- The child has the right to know and be cared for by his or her parents and extended family. Where separation occurs, family reunification must be the primary goal.
- In all actions and decisions concerning children, the parents should expect due process; be notified in advance of potential child apprehension; and be given an opportunity to participate in proceedings.
- Birth alert systems currently being used to trigger the apprehension of an infant should be avoided as much as possible. Instead, emphasis should be given on a range of prenatal services and preventive care, provided this meets the requirements of child safety.
- Indigenous peoples should not be subjected to any act of genocide or violence, including forcibly removing children of the group to another group. Indigenous peoples have the right not to be subjected to forced assimilation or destruction of their culture. (United Nations Declaration on the Rights of Indigenous Peoples, Articles 7&8)
- Due regard should be paid to continuity of a child's upbringing in the child's cultural and linguistic background. In any placement of an Indigenous child, preference should be given to placement with (1) family; (2) a member of the child's extended family; (3) other members of the Indigenous child's community and nation; or (4) other Indigenous families; (5) non-Indigenous families.
- Indigenous families and communities have the right to exercise shared responsibility for the upbringing, training, education and wellbeing of their children. Where Indigenous governments have enacted child welfare laws, these should have precedence.
- Children should not be apprehended on the basis of economic poverty, substandard housing or the health issues of parents or children. The underlying social determinants of health should be addressed to prevent further child apprehension.
- The federal government should support the establishment of guiding principles for Indigenous child wellness and, in collaboration with provinces and territories, publish annual reports on the number of

First Nations, Inuit, and Métis Nation children in care.
(Indigenous Services Canada, 2018

FOOTNOTES

1- Private interviews with twelve aboriginal survivors of three B.C. Indian Residential Schools, from the collection of Rudy and Diana James, Officers, IHRAAM, February 13 – 15, 1998 – Videotaped Testimonies and Written Affidavits

2 - Private interviews with twelve aboriginal survivors of three B.C. Indian Residential Schools, from the collection of Rudy and Diana James, Officers, IHRAAM, February 13 – 15, 1998 – Videotaped Testimonies and Written Affidavits

3- Proceedings of the First International Tribunal into the Canadian Residential Schools, Vancouver, BC, June 12 -14, 1998 (under the auspices of IHRAAM, The International Human Rights Association of American Minorities) – Videotaped testimonies and written affidavits of eyewitness survivors of ten residential schools.

4 - Correspondence and Records of British Columbia Indian Residential Schools, and Reports of the B.C. Superintendent and Indian Agents, 1891 – 1953, in The Archives of the Department of Indian Affairs, Ottawa, RG 10 Series

5 - Graham, J., Swift, K. & Delaney, R. (2012). Canadian Social Policy: An introduction. University of British Columbia.

6 - Sinclair, R. & Grekul, J. (2012). Aboriginal youth gangs in Canada: (de)constructing an epidemic. First
Peoples Child & Family Review, 7(1), 8-28.

7 - Fournier, S. & Crey, E. (1997). Stolen from our embrace: The abduction of First Nations children and the restoration of Aboriginal communities. Vancouver: Douglas & McIntyre.

8 - McKenzie, B. & Hudson, P. (1985). Native children, child welfare, and the colonization of Native people. In Levitt, K. & Wharf, B.

(Eds.), Challenge of child welfare (125-141). Vancouver: University of British Columbia Press.

9 - Statistics Canada. (2013). Aboriginal Peoples in Canada, First Nations People, Métis and Inuit--National
Household Survey, 2011. Ottawa: Minister of Industry. Retrieved from http://www12.statcan.gc.ca/nhs-enm/2011/as-sa/99-011-x/
99-011-x2011001-eng.pdf

10 - Turner, A. (2016). Insights on Canadian society: Living arrangements of Aboriginal children aged 14 and
under. Statistics Canada. Retrieved from http://www.statcan.gc.ca/pub/75-006-
x/2016001/article/14547-eng.htm

11 - Bennett, M., Blackstock, C., & De la Ronde, R. (2005). A literature review and annotated bibliography on aspects of Aboriginal child welfare in Canada (2 nd ed.). Ottawa, First Nations Child and Family Caring Society. Retrieved from http://cwrp.ca/sites/default/files/publications/en/AboriginalCWLitReview_2ndEd.pdf

12 - Gough, P., Trocmé, N., Brown, I., Knoke, D., & Blackstock, C. (2005). Pathways to overrepresentation of Aboriginal children in care. (CECW Information Sheet #23E). Toronto, ON: University of Toronto.

13 - Blackstock, C. (2016, October). Keynote speech at the Reimagining Indigenous child welfare in Canada symposium, Osgoode Hall Law School, Toronto, Ontario.

14 - Sinclair, R. (2016). A genealogical study of Indigenous adoption in Canada: A multifaceted examination of the removal of Indigenous children with a concentration on policy shifts between the years of 1950 and 1985. Informal name - "Pe-kīwēwin Project" (www.pekiwewin.ca). Funded by the Social
Science and Humanities Research Council (Insight Grant 2016-2021)

15 - Canada, Erasmus, G., & Dussault, R. (1996). Report of the Royal Commission on Aboriginal Peoples. Ottawa: The Commission.

16 - Sinclair, R. (2007b). Identity lost and found: Lessons from the sixties scoop. First Peoples Child & Family Review, 3(1), 65-82

17 - UN General Assembly. Convention on the Prevention and Punishment of the Crime of Genocide (1948). Retrieved from http://www.hrweb.org/legal/genocide.html

18 - Kimelman, Justice E. (1985). No quiet place: Review committee on Indian and Métis adoption and placements. Manitoba Community Services.

19 - The Child and Family Services Act of 1985 (Manitoba). C.C.S.M. c. C80. §§ 1-90 (2015)

20 - Sinclair, R. (2016). A genealogical study of Indigenous adoption in Canada: A multifaceted examination of
the removal of Indigenous children with a concentration on policy shifts between the years of
1950 and 1985. Informal name - "Pe-kīwēwin Project" (www.pekiwewin.ca). Funded by the Social
Science and Humanities Research Council (Insight Grant 2016-2021).

11

Suicide

The suicide problem among Indigenous populations in Canada is an ongoing problem of epidemic proportions. Decades of cultural and physical child abuse have taken their toll to such an extent that the government of Canada was forced to take notice. The government study from 2011-2016 reported:

Suicide rates have consistently been shown to be higher among First Nations people, Métis and Inuit in Canada than the rate among non-Indigenous people; however, suicide rates vary by community, Indigenous group, age group and sex. The historical and ongoing impacts of colonization, forced placement of Indigenous children in residential schools in the 19th and 20th centuries, removal of Indigenous children from their families and communities during the "Sixties scoop" and the forced relocation of communities has been well documented. These resulted in the breakdown of families, communities, political and economic structures; loss of language, culture and traditions; exposure to abuse; intergenerational transmission of trauma; and marginalization, which are suggested to be associated with the high rates of suicide. While suicide among Indigenous people has been examined previously, studies were based on a decades-old cohort or used an area-based geo-zones approach. Past studies also examined suicides among only one or two Indigenous groups using the same methodology. Finally, they did not examine suicide among Indigenous people for some geographies such as on and off reserve, rural areas and small, medium and large population centres.

Suicide rates among First Nations people, Métis and Inuit were significantly higher than the rate among non-Indigenous people. The rate among First Nations people (24.3 deaths per 100,000 person-years at risk) was three times higher than the rate among non-Indigenous people (8.0 deaths per 100,000 person-years at risk). Among First Nations people living on reserve, the rate was about twice as high as that among those living off reserve. However, suicide rates varied by First Nations band, with just over 60% of bands having a zero suicide rate. The rate among Métis (14.7Note E: Use with caution deaths per 100,000 person-years at risk) was approximately twice as high as the rate among non-Indigenous people. Among Inuit, the rate was approximately nine times higher than the non-Indigenous rate (72.3 versus 8.0 deaths per 100,000 person-years at risk). Suicide rates and disparities were highest in youth and young adults (15 to 24 years) among First Nations males and Inuit male and females.

The high rates of suicide among First Nations people, Métis and Inuit has been suggested to be the result of historical and intergenerational trauma experienced as a result of colonization and on-going marginalization. Colonialism has also been suggested to broadly impact Indigenous peoples' health by producing social, political and economic inequalities that, in turn, play a role in the development of conditions related to poorer health. Many historical and contemporary factors have been associated with suicide among Indigenous people in Canada. These include acculturation stresses like

(1) loss of land, traditional subsistence activities and control over living conditions;
(2) suppression of belief systems and spirituality;
(3) weakening of social and political institutions;
(4) racial discrimination; and
(5) marginalization.

(Statistics Canada, 2018. p.5 - 6)

Chart 1
Age-specific suicide rates (number of deaths by suicide per 100,000 person-years at risk) among First Nations males living on reserve and non-Indigenous males in Canada, household population aged 1 year or older, Canada, 2011-2016

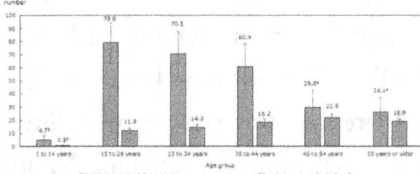

(Statistics Canada, 2018. p. 9)

Chart 2
Age-specific suicide rates (number of deaths by suicide per 100,000 person-years at risk) among Inuit males in Inuit Nunangat and non-Indigenous males in Canada, household population aged 1 year or older, Canada, 2011-2016

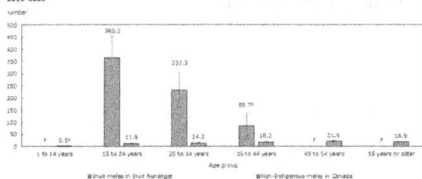

(Statistics Canada, 2018. p. 11)

Of particular concern is the high rate of suicide among Indigenous children under 15. The suicide rate among First Nations boys, nationally, was four times higher than among non-Indigenous boys. It was ten times higher among First Nations boys living on reserve. As with other national trends, this rate may obscure regional differences. Previous reports have suggested that in some remote First Nations communities in Ontario, under-15 suicide rates were nearly 50 times higher than non-Indigenous rates. And, among Inuit communities of Nunatsiavut, the age-specific disparity was largest among 10 to 19-year-olds relative to their non-Indigenous counterparts outside Inuit Nunangat. Also, rate of death by suicide among Inuit children 10 to 14 years of age appears to be increasing since 1989 although significant fluctuations are seen across time. In line with these rates among children, suicidal ideation among grade 5 to 8 school children in Saskatoon was nearly twice as high among Indigenous children as non-Indigenous children after accounting for mental health, cognitive abilities and bullying experiences. While risk factors for suicide among children are numerous and complex, a recent report suggests that Inuit children and youth in Nunavut experience a lack of mental health services that are specific to them, culturally relevant and of adequate quality. (Statistics Canada, 2018. p. 12)

If we continue to ignore the century and a half of cultural and (arguably) actual genocide perpetuated on the Indigenous Peoples of Canada, most of all on Indigenous children, we will continue to fall short in change. Trauma inflicted at such young ages creates cyclical and toxic cycles that will continue to manifest in different, but predictably destructive ways. Now we can add generations crippled with suicidal depression to the list of government crimes against Indigenous children.

12

Missing and Murdered Indigenous Women

Another problem plaguing the Indigenous populations of Canada is that of the Missing and Murdered Indigenous Women. This is another issue that Indigenous woman must deal with besides the childhood trauma passed down from multiple generations of abuse at the hands of the Canadian government and the church, sex trafficking, and increased risk due to higher levels of substance abuse in response to aforementioned high levels of trauma within the population. The following facts are reported by Canadian Department of Justice:

Indigenous women represent 10% of the total population of missing women in Canada. According to the Missing and Murdered Aboriginal Women: 2015 Update to the National Operational Overview report by the Royal Canadian Mounted Police, Indigenous women represent 10% (174) of the total population of women in Canada missing for at least 30 days reported by the Canadian Police Information Centre (CPIC) (1,750). Of these, 111 women were identified as missing due to "unknown" circumstances or foul play was suspected. Proportion of Indigenous women homicide victims increased since 1991.

Between 1980 and 2014, there were 6,849 police-reported female homicide cases in Canada. Among the total number of female victims, 16% were Indigenous women. Since 1991, the number of murdered non-indigenous women has declined. In contrast, the number of murdered Indigenous women has remained relatively stable, thus accounting for an increasing proportion of Indigenous female homicide victims. For example, in 1980, Indigenous women accounted for 9% (18) of female homicide victims, whereas in 2014, they accounted for 21% (30) of female homicide victims. In 2014, the rate of homicide of Indigenous women (3.64 per 100,000) was almost six times higher than non-Indigenous women (0.65 per 100,000).

The prairies also had a higher police-reported homicide rate of Indigenous women than the overall rate in Canada. The largest difference in police-reported homicide rates between Indigenous women and non-Indigenous women was in the Yukon (12 times higher for Indigenous women) and in Saskatchewan (11 times higher for Indigenous women). Half of the homicides of Indigenous women were committed by a family member.

Of the total solved homicide cases of Indigenous women between 1980 and 2014, half (53%) were committed by a family member, a quarter (26%) by an acquaintance and 8% by strangers. The 2014 homicide survey found that fewer homicides of Indigenous women occurred in a residence (66%) compared to non-Indigenous women (88%). In addition, 17% of homicides of Indigenous women occurred on a street, a road, or a highway compared to 1% of non-Indigenous women. (Department of Justice Canada, 2017)

While we do need to be cautious when making comparisons on such small numbers in Canada, taking a brief look at some of the statistics from our southern neighbors, the United States, helps to bring the epidemic against Indigenous women in North America into proportion. This from www.nativewomenswilderness.org:

- Indigenous Women (girls +) murdered 10x higher than all other ethnicities.
- Murder is the 3rd leading cause of death for Indigenous Women (Centers for Disease Control).

- More than 4 out of 5 Indigenous Women have experienced violence (84.3%) (National Institute of Justice Report).
- More than half Indigenous Women experience sexual violence (56.1%).
- More than half Indigenous Women have been physically abused by their intimate partners (55.5%).
- Less than half of Indigenous Women have been stalked in their lifetime (48.8%).
- Indigenous Women are 1.7 times more likely than Anglo-American women to experience violence.
- Indigenous Women are 2 times more likely to be raped than Anglo-American white women.
- Murder rate of Indigenous Women is 3 times higher than Anglo-American women.

Being an Indigenous woman in North America is one of the least, if not the least, physically safe demographics. I encourage the reader to check out the full report of the national inquiry at https://www.mmiwg-ffada.ca/

- More than [illegible] of Indigenous Women have experienced violence [illegible] (National Institute of Justice Report).
- More than half of Indigenous Women experience sexual violence [illegible].
- More than half of Indigenous Women [illegible] physically abused by [illegible] intimate partner [illegible].
- [illegible] of Indigenous Women have been [illegible] in their lifetime [illegible].
- Indigenous Women are [illegible] times more likely than [illegible] American [illegible] to experience violence.
- Indigenous Women [illegible] than any other [illegible] American white women.
- [illegible] rate of Indigenous Women [illegible] times higher than [illegible] American women.

[illegible] Indigenous Women in North America [illegible] the [illegible] physically [illegible] the reader [illegible] check out the full report [illegible] National Institute of [illegible] community [illegible].

13

"Starlight Tours"

Jim Maddin was on the Saskatoon police force for 25 years. Now he sits on city council.

"If somebody asked me does this happen. I couldn't look them in the eye and say absolutely no, it's never happened; never will happen. I couldn't say that," Maddin says. "General talk, discussion, locker room, coffee talk, what have you. Reference made to that. I've heard stories of people where this has happened to in other cities. Who's to say it didn't happen here? I can't say it didn't happen, but I can also say that I never observed it personally at all. And at no time when I was in charge of officers on the street, at no time was it ever brought to my attention."

"Officers, I think, can tend to get frustrated with it, sure because they don't tend to see the system actually contributing to the solution of the problem," Maddin says. "It's just a simple temporary fix to pick up the intoxicated person, get them out of the public view or off the public street until such time they're sobered up to better care for themselves and then release them back, only to repeat it again. Sometimes in a very short time -- a matter of hours." (Brass, 2004)

The Saskatoon freezing deaths were a series of (alleged) murders involving Indigenous men and Saskatoon Police officers in the early 2000's. The officers would arrest Indigenous people, usually men, for alleged drunkenness, sometimes without cause. The officers would then (allegedly) drive them to the outskirts of the city at night in the winter, take their clothing, and abandon them, leaving them stranded in sub-zero temperatures.

Reports of the practice date back to at least 1976. As of 2021, despite convictions for related offences, no Saskatoon police officer has been convicted specifically for having caused freezing deaths. The three known victims to have succumb to hypothermia are Rodney Naistus, Lawrence Wegner, and Neil Stonechild.

Timeline

An overview the events surrounding the death of Neil Stonechild and the subsequent inquiry.

- Nov. 24, 1990 - Neil Stonechild(17) and Jason Roy leave a house party around midnight in temperatures around -25C.
- Nov. 25, 1990 - Roy is stopped by constables Brad Senger and Larry Hartwig. States they have Stonechild in the back seat, and he is bloodied, screaming for help and yelling that the police were going to kill him.
- Nov. 29, 1990 – Stonechild's frozen body is discovered. Sgt. Keith Jarvis of the morality unit is assigned to investigate.
- Dec. 3, 1990 - Stonechild's funeral is held. Family observe two parallel cuts on the bridge of his nose.
- Dec. 5, 1990 - Jarvis concludes the Stonechild file. His report doesn't address the missing shoe, how he walked nine km in a snowstorm, or how he incurred cuts on his nose.

Roy's statement that he saw Stonechild in the back of Senger's and Hartwig's cruiser is excluded from the report.
- March 4, 1991 – It is reported that Stonechild's family disagree with Jarvis's report and suspect foul play.
- June 4, 1997 – A fictional article in the Saskatoon Sun, by constable Brian Trainor, describes two cops who pick up a drunk and leave him outside the city.

- 1998 (exact date unkown) - The original file in-vestigating Neil Stonechild's death is destroyed by the department during a routine purging of old files.
- Jan. 29, 2000 - The body of Indigenous man, Rod-ney Nais-tus, is discovered on the city outskirts.
- Feb. 3, 2000 – Another Indigenous man, Lawrence Wegner, has his frozen body is discovered in the same area. Aboriginal man Darrell Night tells police that two officers abandoned him in the same area on a recent cold night.
- Feb. 22, 2000 - Reports surface that connects Night's allega-tions with Stonechild's death, nearly a decade earlier.
- Sept. 20, 2001 - Two police officers who admitted to abandon-ing Darrell Night in freezing temperatures are fired.
- Feb. 20, 2003 – A public Inquiry is announced into Stonechild's death.
- Sept. 8, 2003 - Commission begins, headed by commissioner Justice David Wright.
- Jan. 9, 2004 - Police officials announce that all city cruisers will be GPS equipped.
- May 18, 2004 - Saskatoon police admit that the 1990 inves-tigation into Stonechild's death was inade-quate, former police chief Russell Sabo apologizes to Stonechild's family.
- Oct. 26, 2004 - The Stonechild inquiry finds Stone-child was in the custody of Senger and Hartwig on the night he died, and that injuries on his nose were likely made by handcuffs.
- November 2004 - Senger and Hartwig are fired.
- June 19, 2008 - Senger and Hartwig's appeal is denied.
- Dec. 18, 2008 - Senger's and Hartwig's applica-tions to appeal denied. Neither will ever spend a day in jail. Both deny involve-ment to this day.

[illegible] the original file investigating [illegible] by the detectives [illegible] old file.

[illegible] 2007: The body [illegible] found [illegible]

[illegible] Nicholas [illegible] as [illegible] doned [illegible]

[illegible] [illegible] not [illegible] tracked [illegible]

[illegible] 2011: Two officers [illegible]

[illegible] advanced [illegible] moratorium [illegible]

Jan. 9, 2014: [illegible] announced [illegible] decided [illegible]

May 18, 2016: [illegible] court [illegible] 1990 [illegible] was [illegible] under [illegible]

[illegible] 2016: The [illegible] in the community [illegible] and [illegible]

[illegible] 2017 [illegible] and Harwig [illegible]

Feb. 12, [illegible] appeal is denied.

[illegible] 2018: [illegible] Both [illegible] involvement [illegible]

Legislation, Reports, and Inquiries

14

Highlights from the Indian Act

One of the most famous examples of this oppression and subsequent resistance and adaptation is known as the "Potlatch Law." In 1884, the federal government banned potlatches under the Indian Act, with other ceremonies such as the sun dance to follow in the coming years. The potlatch was one of the most important ceremonies for coastal First Nations in Western Canada, and marked important occasions as well as serving a crucial role in the distribution of wealth.

"Every Indian or other person who engages in or assists in celebrating the Indian festival known as the "Potlatch" or in the Indian dance known as the "Tamanawas" is guilty of a misdemeanor, and liable to imprisonment for a term of not more than six nor less than two months in any gaol or other place of confinement; and every Indian or persons who encourages ... an Indian to get up such a festival ... shall be liable to the same punishment" (Indian Act, 1885.)

The following quote is from Judge Alfred Scow, Royal Commission of Aboriginal Peoples (RCAP),

"The Indian Act did a very destructive thing in outlawing the ceremonials. This provision of the Indian Act was in place for close to 75 years and what that did was it prevented the passing down of our oral history. It prevented the passing down of our values. It meant the interruption of the respected forms of government be they oral and not in writing before any of the Europeans came to this country. We had a system that worked for us. We respected each other. We had ways of dealing with disputes. We did not have institutions like the courts that we are talking about now. We did not have the massive bureaucracies that are in place today that we have to go through in order to get some kind of recognition and come kind of redsolution." (Scow, 1992)

Introduction of Pass Requirement to leave Reserve

Credit - F. Laurie Barron, Department of Native Studies University of Saskatchewan

"In the aftermath of the North-West Rebellion, Indian Affairs instituted a pass system designed to confine Indians to their reserves in selected areas of the prairie west. Where the system was in effect, an Indian wishing to leave his reserve was required to obtain a pass, duly signed by the Indian agent and stipulating the duration and purpose of the leave. Indians without a pass, or in violation of the terms of the pass, were taken into custody by the police and summarily returned to their reserve. Lacking any basis in law, the system evolved as a form of local administrative tyranny, informally endorsed at the ministerial level of Indian Affairs. It aimed at a racial segregation meant to restrain Indian mobility, thereby minimizing friction with the white community, as well as ameliorating certain real or imagined problems, such as Indian prostitution, alcoholism, and cattle killing.

From the beginning, the system was ineffectual. While Indians either ignored or openly defied the restrictions, the North West Mounted Police eventually came to the conclusion that, without legislative sanction, passes could not and should not be enforced. Faced with this situation, Indian Affairs by the early 1890s had no choice but to modify the scheme, both in substance and in intent. Although Indian agents continued to maintain the pretense that a pass was necessary for those wishing to leave the reserve, in practice passes were now granted almost on demand and for every conceivable purpose. The system was no longer meant to serve as an instrument of confinement, but merely as a means of monitoring Indian movement. Passes survived into the twentieth century and were used in some areas as late as the 1930s. But they never became the kind of repressive mechanism they were intended to be." (Barron,1988. p. 25)

Inability of Indians to vote

The following is from Elections Canada, A Brief History of Federal Voting Rights in Canada:

1876 Indian Act - First Nations peoples' lives are governed by the Indian Act. It grants First Nations peoples the right to vote, but only if they give up their Indian status. They can vote because the law no longer considers them "Indians."

1917   Wartime Elections Act and Military Voters Act - During the First World War, all male and female members of the armed forces and female relatives of soldiers are offered the right to vote. This is the first time that some women, some men under the age of 21, and some First Nations peoples can vote in a Canadian federal election.

1918   - Many women can vote federally. Canadian women now have the right to vote in federal elections if they meet the same eligibility criteria as men.

1920 Dominion Elections Act - A new elections law brings in major changes, such as the appointment of a Chief Electoral Officer, but does not provide consistent voting rights across Canada. Those disqualified from voting in their home province because of their race are ineligible to vote in federal elections. (For example, since British Columbia excludes Asian Canadians from voting provincially, they cannot vote federally. However, Asian Canadians living elsewhere do have the federal vote.) Across Canada, First Nations people living on reserves are not eligible to vote.

1934 Inuit are disqualified - Legislation specifically excludes Inuit from voting in federal elections.

1948 All Asian Canadians gain the vote - The federal vote is now open to Canadians regardless of provincial exclusions. (Japanese, Chinese and other Asian Canadians can vote federally, no matter which province they live in.)

1950 Inuit are able to vote - Inuit obtain the right to vote in Canadian federal elections.

1960 First Nations women and men can vote - First Nations women and men are able to vote no matter where they live and without giving up their Indian status.

1982 Canadian Charter of Rights and Freedoms - The Canadian Charter of Rights and Freedoms affirms the right of every Canadian citizen to vote and to stand as a candidate. (Elections Canada, 2021)

Creation of Reserves

The following is from The Canadian Encyclopedia:

Reserve means a tract of land, the legal title to which is vested in Her Majesty, that has been set apart by Her Majesty for the use and benefit of a band (of Indians). The important thing to consider is that Indigenous peoples in Canada never own any of the land allotted to them as reserves. In alignment with the original intent of the Indian Act for assimilation of the Indigenous into settler society, all "Indian land" in Canada is, in fact government or "Crown" land on loan until assimilation. Also worth considering that the government of Canada owns over eighty-eight percent of all land in Canada, with over half of the remainder going to massive corporations. The Indigenous peoples get nothing.

6. All lands reserved for Indians or for any tribe, band or body of Indians, or held in trust for their benefit, shall be deemed to be reserved and held for the same purposes as before the passing of this Act, but subject to its provisions; and no such lands shall be sold, alienated or leased until they have been released or surrendered to the Crown for the purposes of this Act.

9. Upon the death of any Indian holding under location or other duly recognized title any lot or parcel of land, the right and interest therein of such deceased Indian shall, together with his goods and chattels, devolve one-third upon his widow, and the remainder upon his children equally ; and such children shall have a like estate in such land as their father ; but should such Indian die without issue but leaving

a widow, such lot or parcel of land and his goods and chattels shall be vested in her, and if he leaves no widow, then in the Indian nearest akin to the deceased, but if he have no heir nearer than a cousin, then the same shall be vested in the Crown for the benefit of the band : But whatever may be the final disposition of the land, the claimant or claimants shall not be held to be legally in possession until they obtain a location ticket from the Superintendent-General in the manner prescribed in the case of new locations.

46. In the case of an Indian reserve which adjoins or is situated wholly or partly within an incorporated town or city having a population of not less than eight thousand ... the Governor in Council may, upon the recommendation of the Superintendent General, refer to the judge of the Exchequer Court of Canada for inquiry and report the question as to whether it is expedient, having regard to the interest of the public and of the Indians of the band for whose use the reserve is held, that the Indians should be removed from the reserve or any part of it....

The reserve system is governed by the Indian Act and relates to First Nations, bands and people, referred to in a legal context as Indians. Inuit and Métis people normally do not live on reserves, though many live in communities that are governed by land claims, or self-government agreements.

Under the Indian Act, an Indian Reserve is land held by the Crown "for the use and benefit of the respective bands for which they were set apart" under treaties or other agreements. Many First Nations (Indian Bands) include several separate portions of land as their reserve. Only those with Registered Indian status (i.e., Status Indians), may 'own' land on a reserve, though such ownership remains at the discretion of the federal government, and does not entail full legal possession. Certificates of Possession, often referred to as CPs, convey "ownership" of reserve lands to their holders but they lack the legal status of deeds. Furthermore, not all bands have reserves. The Caldwell First Nation in

Ontario does not have a reserve, nor do several bands in Newfoundland. (McCue, 2011)

Prohibition of Solicitation of funds for Indian legal claims

In the early 1900's, the Nisga'a First Nation would attempt to take a legal route to attempt to secure their traditional territory. Any and all attempts were denied by the governments of British Columbia and/or ignored by the Canadian Government. A 1927 amendment (Section 141) forbade any First Nation or Indian band from retaining legal counsel for the purpose of making a claim against the governments, and further forbade them from raising money to retain counsel, on threat of imprisonment:

> Every person who, without the consent of the Superintendent General expressed in writing, receives, obtains, solicits or requests from any Indian any payment or contribution or promise of any payment or contribution for the purpose of raising a fund or providing money for the prosecution of any claim which the tribe or band of Indians to which such Indian belongs, or of which he is a member, has or is represented to have for the recovery of any claim or money for the benefit of the said tribe or band, shall be guilty of an offence an liable upon summary conviction for each such offence to a penalty not exceeding two hundred dollars and not less than fifty dollars or to imprisonment for any term not exceeding two months. (Indian Act, Section 141, 1876 – Repealed 1951)

Without access to the court system to resolve land claim disagreements, the Indigenous peoples were completely at the mercy of the government of Canada and the Indian agents' predatory actions and legislation. The right to representation is a hallmark of western civilization, but one not granted to the Indigenous of Canada until the last half of the twentieth century.

15

UN Report on Indigenous Rights

"The United Nations Declaration on the Rights of Indigenous Peoples (UNDRIP) was adopted by the General Assembly on Thursday, 13 September 2007, by a majority of 144 states in favour, 4 votes against (Australia, Canada, New Zealand and the United States) and 11 abstentions (Azerbaijan, Bangladesh, Bhutan, Burundi, Colombia, Georgia, Kenya, Nigeria, Russian Federation, Samoa and Ukraine).

Years later the four countries that voted against have reversed their position and now support the UN Declaration.

Today the Declaration is the most comprehensive international instrument on the rights of indigenous peoples. It establishes a universal framework of minimum standards for the survival, dignity, and well-being of the indigenous peoples of the world and it elaborates on existing human rights standards and fundamental freedoms as they apply to the specific situation of indigenous peoples. (United Nations Declaration on the Rights of Indigenous Peoples, 2007)

[illegible]

[illegible] United Nations [illegible] Human Rights [illegible] (UDHR) was adopted [illegible] Australia [illegible] in favour [illegible] Canada, New Zealand and the United [illegible] and [illegible] Saudi Arabia [illegible]

[illegible] Declaration.

[illegible] the Declaration [illegible] international [illegible] framework of [illegible] human rights [illegible] adopted [illegible] languages [illegible]

16

The White Paper 1969

From the paper Statement of the Government of Canada on Indian Policy, 1969. Presented to the First Session of the Twenty-eighth Parliament by the Honourable Jean Chrétien, Minister of Indian Affairs and Northern Development:

"To be an Indian is to be a man, with all a man's needs and abilities.

To be an Indian is also to be different. It is to speak different languages, draw different pictures, tell different tales and to rely on a set of values developed in a different world.

Canada is richer for its Indian component, although there have been times diversity seemed of little value to many Canadians.

But to be a Canadian Indian today is to be someone different in another way. It is to be someone apart - apart in law, apart in the provision of government services and, too often, part in social contacts.

To be an Indian is to lack power - the power to act as owner of your lands, the power to spend your own money and, too often, the power to change your own condition.

Not always, but too often, to be an Indian is to be without - without a job, a good house, or running water; without knowledge, training or technical skill
and, above all, without those feelings of dignity and self-confidence that a man must have if he is to walk with his head held high.

All these conditions of the Indians are the product of history and have nothing to do with their abilities and capacities. Indian relations with other Canadians began with special treatment by government and

society, and special treatment has been the rule since Europeans first settled in Canada. Special treatment has made of the Indians a community disadvantaged and apart.
Obviously, the course of history must be changed". (Government of Canada, 1969)

Obviously, the course of history must be changed, but changed how? And for whose benefit? What was wrapped inside the 24 page document presented under the cloak of anti-discrimination and equal status amounted to nothing short of cultural genocide. Indian reserves would be (further) sold by the federal government into private ownership, all Indians would lose their Indian Status and be assimilated into the Canadian population, and what little independence and commitment to culture that was enjoyed by the Indians was quickly to evaporate. None of the existing treaties would continue to be honoured and no further discussions on land or harvesting rights would be entertained.

This was in many ways the opposite of what most of Canada's Indigenous families were hoping for. They had been dealing with the state taking away their children, at gunpoint if necessary, and watching the church and the state continue to steal their culture and education via residential schools and assimilationist policies. With one document the federal government hoped to end its "Indian Problem" once and for all. While the Indigenous hoped to take back their own education and self-governance it became suddenly apparent that a century of oppression and cultural destruction was far from over.

Harold Cardinal, Cree writer, political leader, teacher, negotiator, and lawyer was one of few university educated Indigenous People in the country in the late 1960's. His education and well-spoken demeanor quickly elevated him to the position of leader of the Indian Association of Alberta, a position he would be voted in to at the tender age of 23 and hold for an impressive nine terms. Cardinal quickly became a voice for change and activism as well as Chief of the Sucker Creek Indian Band. After Trudeau's government consulted with first nations from across the country, promising a move towards self-governance and honouring treaty rights, the paper proposed the opposite. Cardinal was outraged and later had this to say.

"We do not want the Indian Act retained because it is a good piece of legislation. It isn't. It is discriminatory from start to finish. But it is a lever in our hands and an embarrassment to the government, as it should be. No just society and no society with even pretensions to being just can long tolerate such a piece of legislation, but we would rather continue to live in bondage under the inequitable Indian Act than surrender our sacred rights. Any time the government wants to honour its obligations to us we are more than happy to help devise new Indian legislation." (Cardinal, 1999)

Consider this, though a racist and oppressive document, The Indian Act is the sole piece of existing legislation ensuring any Indigenous rights. And giving it up meant surrendering any existing legislative claims to special Indigenous rights as there were no other policies or documentation but the Indian Act that ensured such rights. Where the government thought it had a splintered opponent it quickly discovered that the recent world wars in which thousands of Indigenous had served, even without Canadian citizenship had the twofold effect of opening up communication between the different bands across the country and opening up the eyes of Canadians and Indigenous alike to growing recognition of human rights.

The white paper would prove to not only be a huge misstep and ultimately a failure and embarrassment for the Canadian government, but it would also prove to unite and empower the Indigenous communities from across the country. Trudeau, in a famous statement, claimed that native rights could not be recognized because "no society can be built on historical might-have-been's."

Further, Trudeau said, "We'll keep them in the ghetto as long as they want." The response would be the "Red Paper" which we will get too next and the rise of protesting and activism in the Indigenous community. In 1970 Blue Quill Residential School would be occupied by the parents of Indigenous children for 17 days of peaceful protest before ultimately evicting the church presence completely from the school, becoming the first Indigenous run school in Canada.

17

The Red Paper

Harold Cardinal's Indian Association of Alberta responded in 1970 with a paper of their own titled "Citizens Plus" which became known as the Red Paper. The 94 page Red Paper was a counter-proposal to the White Paper. On January 22, 1970, the Indian Chiefs of Alberta sent a letter of concern addressed to Pierre Trudeau, in which they stated:

"This assembly of all the Indian Chiefs of Alberta is deeply concerned with the action taken by the Minister of Indian Affairs and Northern Development, the Honorable Jean Chretien, regarding the implementation of the Indian policy. Time and time again, on the one hand, the Minister has declared publicly to the Canadian people that the Indian Policy contained proposals to be discussed with the Indian people. On the other hand, Indian Affairs officials have been recruited for implementation teams to go ahead with the implementation of the policy paper.

We find this double-headed approach contradictory. A glaring example is the appointment of the Claims Commissioner. Another example is the concentrated public relations program being conducted to impose the White Paper on the Canadian public. We find this incompatible with the Just Society. Discussions between the Federal department of Indian Affairs and provincial governments have also initiated. This assembly of all the Indian Chiefs of Alberta reaffirms its position of unity and recognizes the Indian Association of Alberta as the voice of all the Treaty Indian people of this province.

"As representatives of our people we are pledged to continue our earnest efforts to preserve the hereditary and legal privileges of our people. At this meeting of Alberta Indian Chiefs, we have reviewed the first draft of our Counter Policy to the Chretien paper. We plan to 192 aboriginal policy studies complete our final draft in the near future, for presentation to the Federal Government. We request that no further process of implementation takes place and that action already taken be reviewed to minimize suspicions and to make possible a positive and constructive dialogue between your government and our people". (Indian Chiefs of Alberta, 1970)

In June of 1970 the Chiefs made good on their promise by publishing their 94-page response to the 1969 white paper. While the white paper proposed abolition, the red paper favoured reformation. While the White paper promised to "give credit" to Indian cultural contributions to Canadian society, the Red paper insisted the only way to continue to appreciate Indian culture was to continue to be Indians. With little left of the original treaties left already, giving up the rest and assimilating fully into western society was too much. For the first time in decades organized pushback caused the Federal Government to formally withdrawal the white paper in 1970. The preamble for the Red paper says:

"To us who are Treaty Indians there is nothing more important than our Treaties, our lands and the well-being of our future generation. We have studied carefully the contents of the Government White Paper on Indians and we have concluded that it offers despair instead of hope. Under the guise of land ownership, the government has devised a scheme whereby within a generation or shortly after the proposed Indian Lands Act expires our people would be left with no land and consequently the future generation would be condemned to the despair and ugly spectre of urban poverty in ghettos.

In Alberta, we have told the Federal Minister of Indian Affairs that we do not wish to discuss his White Paper with him until we reach a position where we can bring forth viable alternatives because we know that his paper is wrong and that it will harm our people. We refused to meet him on his White Paper because we have been stung and hurt by his concept of consultation. 190 aboriginal policy studies. In his White Paper, the Minister said, "This review was a response to things said by Indian people at the consultation meetings which began a year ago and culminated in a meeting in Ottawa in April."

Yet, what Indians asked for land ownership that would result in Provincial taxation of our reserves? What Indians asked that the Canadian Constitution be changed to remove any reference to Indians or Indian lands? What Indians asked that Treaties be brought to an end? What group of Indians asked that aboriginal rights not be recognized? What group of Indians asked for a Commissioner whose purview would exclude half of the Indian population in Canada?

The answer is no Treaty Indians asked for any of these things and yet through his concept of "consultation," the Minister said that his White Paper was in response to things said by Indians.

We felt that with this concept of consultation held by the Minister and his department, that if we met with them to discuss the contents of his White Paper without being fully prepared, that even if we just talked about the weather, he would turn around and tell Parliament and the Canadian public that we accepted his White Paper." (Indian Chiefs of Alberta, 1970)

18

Truth and Reconciliation

The Truth and Reconciliation Commission (TRC) of Canada was a commission active in Canada from 2008 to 2015, organized by the parties of the Indian Residential Schools Settlement Agreement. Their mandate states:

There is an emerging and compelling desire to put the events of the past behind us so that we can
work towards a stronger and healthier future. The truth telling and reconciliation process as part of an overall holistic and comprehensive response to the Indian Residential School legacy is a sincere indication and acknowledgement of the injustices and harms experienced by Aboriginal people and the need for continued healing. This is a profound commitment to establishing new relationships embedded in mutual recognition and respect that will forge a brighter future. The truth of our common experiences will help set our spirits free and pave the way to reconciliation.
Principals
Through the Agreement, the Parties have agreed that an historic Truth and Reconciliation Commission will be established to contribute to truth, healing and reconciliation. The Truth and Reconciliation Commission will build upon the "Statement of Reconciliation" dated January 7, 1998 and the principles developed by the Working Group on Truth and Reconciliation and of the Exploratory Dialogues (1998-1999). These principles are as follows: accessible; victim-centered;

confidentiality (if required by the former student); do no harm; health and safety of participants; representative; public/transparent; accountable; open and honourable process; comprehensive; inclusive, educational, holistic, just and fair; respectful; voluntary; flexible; and forward looking in terms of rebuilding and renewing Aboriginal relationships and the relationship between Aboriginal and non-Aboriginal Canadians.

Reconciliation is an ongoing individual and collective process, and will require commitment from
all those affected including First Nations, Inuit and Métis former Indian Residential School (IRS) students, their families, communities, religious entities, former school employees, government and the people of Canada. Reconciliation may occur between any of the above groups.

The goals of the Commission shall be to:

a)   Acknowledge Residential School experiences, impacts and consequences;

b)   Provide a holistic, culturally appropriate and safe setting for former students, their families and communities as they come forward to the Commission;

c)   Witness,' support, promote and facilitate truth and reconciliation events at both the national and community levels;

d)   Promote awareness and public education of Canadians about the IRS system and its impacts;

e)   Identify sources and create as complete an historical record as possible of the IRS system and legacy. The record shall be preserved and made accessible to the public for future study and use;

f)   Produce and submit to the Parties of the Agreement a report including recommendations to the Government of Canada concerning the IRS system and experience including: the history, purpose, operation and supervision of the IRS system, the effect and consequences of IRS

g)   (including systemic harms, intergenerational consequences and the impact on human dignity) and the ongoing legacy of the residential schools;

h) Support commemoration of former Indian Residential School students and their families in accordance with the Commemoration Policy Directive" (TRC Canada, 2021)

Established in June of 2008, The Commission was tasked with the objective of documenting the history and long-lasting impacts of Canada's Residential School System. It travelled across the country allowing survivors to share their stories and accounts both publicly and privately. The Commission emphasizes its priority of education for the tens of millions of Canadians who have been hidden from the truth of these matters.

In June 2015, the TRC released thousands of pages of reports, testimonies, and correspondence summarized into an executive report. It highlighted 94 "calls to action" toward finding a path to reconciliation between Canada and its Indigenous population. The TRC dissolved, completing that phase of its mission in late 2015. The commission published a multi-volume final report that concluded the school system amounted to cultural genocide. Shortly prior to the commission's end, The National Centre for Truth and Reconciliation opened, and stands today as an archive of the research, documents, and testimony collected during the course of the TRC's operation.

TRC Calls to Action Report
From the Truth and Reconciliation Commission Report published in 2015:

Here are the 94 Calls to Action, with points from the articles from the UN resolution tied in for reference. In order to redress the legacy of residential schools and advance the process of Canadian reconciliation, the Truth and Reconciliation Commission makes the following calls to action.

TRC "Calls to Action"
Child welfare

- 1. We call upon the federal, provincial, territorial, and Aboriginal governments to commit to reducing the number of Aboriginal children in care by:
- i. Monitoring and assessing neglect investigations.

ii. Providing adequate resources to enable Aboriginal communities and child-welfare organizations to keep Aboriginal families together where it is safe to do so, and to keep children in culturally appropriate environments, regardless of where they reside.

iii. Ensuring that social workers and others who conduct child-welfare investigations are properly educated and trained about the history and impacts of residential schools.

iv. Ensuring that social workers and others who conduct child-welfare investigations are properly educated and trained about the potential for Aboriginal communities and families to provide more appropriate solutions to family healing.

v. Requiring that all child-welfare decision makers consider the impact of the residential school experience on children and their caregivers.

- 2. We call upon the federal government, in collaboration with the provinces and territories, to prepare and publish annual reports on the number of Aboriginal children who are in care, compared with non-Aboriginal children, as well as the reasons for apprehension, the total spending on preventive and care services by child-welfare agencies, and the effectiveness of various interventions.
- 3. We call upon all levels of government to fully implement Jordan's Principle.
- 4. We call upon the federal government to enact Aboriginal child-welfare legislation that establishes national standards for

Aboriginal child apprehension and custody cases and includes principles that ...

- i. Affirm the right of Aboriginal governments to establish and maintain their own child-welfare agencies.
  ii. Require all child-welfare agencies and courts to take the residential school legacy into account in their decision making.
  iii. Establish, as an important priority, a requirement that placements of Aboriginal children into temporary and permanent care be culturally appropriate.
- 5. We call upon the federal, provincial, territorial, and Aboriginal governments to develop culturally appropriate parenting programs for Aboriginal families.
- Education
- 6. We call upon the Government of Canada to repeal Section 43 of the Criminal Code of Canada.
- 7. We call upon the federal government to develop with Aboriginal groups a joint strategy to eliminate educational and employment gaps between Aboriginal and non-Aboriginal Canadians.
- 8. We call upon the federal government to eliminate the discrepancy in federal education funding for First Nations children being educated on reserves and those First Nations children being educated off reserves.
- 9. We call upon the federal government to prepare and publish annual reports comparing funding for the education of First Nations children on and off reserves, as well as educational and income attainments of Aboriginal peoples in Canada compared with non-Aboriginal people.
- 10. We call on the federal government to draft new Aboriginal education legislation with the full participation and informed consent of Aboriginal peoples. The new legislation would include a commitment to sufficient funding and would incorporate the following principles:

i. Providing sufficient funding to close identified educational achievement gaps within one generation.

ii. Improving educational attainment levels and success rates.

iii. Developing culturally appropriate curricula.

iv. Protecting the right to Aboriginal languages, including the teaching of Aboriginal languages as credit courses.

v. Enabling parental and community responsibility, control, and accountability, similar to what parents enjoy in public school systems.

vi. Enabling parents to fully participate in the education of their children.

vii. Respecting and honoring Treaty relationships.

- 11. We call upon the federal government to provide adequate funding to end the backlog of First Nations students seeking a post-secondary education.
- 12. We call upon the federal, provincial, territorial, and Aboriginal governments to develop culturally appropriate early childhood education programs for Aboriginal families.
- Language and Culture
- 13. We call upon the federal government to acknowledge that Aboriginal rights include Aboriginal language rights.
- 14. We call upon the federal government to enact an Aboriginal Languages Act that incorporates the following principles:

i. Aboriginal languages are a fundamental and valued element of Canadian culture and society, and there is an urgency to preserve them.

ii. Aboriginal language rights are reinforced by the Treaties.

iii. The federal government has a responsibility to provide sufficient funds for Aboriginal-language revitalization and preservation.

iv. The preservation, revitalization, and strengthening of Aboriginal languages and cultures are best managed by Aboriginal people and communities.

v. Funding for Aboriginal language initiatives must reflect the diversity of Aboriginal languages.
- 15. We call upon the federal government to appoint, in consultation with Aboriginal groups, an Aboriginal Languages Commissioner.
- 16. We call upon post-secondary institutions to create university and college degree and diploma programs in Aboriginal languages.
- 17. We call upon all levels of government to enable residential school survivors and their families to reclaim names changed by the residential school system by waiving administrative costs for a period of five years for the name-change process and the revision of official identity documents, such as birth certificates, passports, driver's licenses, health cards, status cards, and social insurance numbers.
- Health
- 18. We call upon the federal, provincial, territorial, and Aboriginal governments to acknowledge that the current state of Aboriginal health in Canada is a direct result of previous Canadian government policies, including residential schools, and to recognize and implement the health-care rights of Aboriginal people as identified in international law, constitutional law, and under the Treaties.
- 19. We call upon the federal government, in consultation with Aboriginal peoples, to establish measurable goals to identify and close the gaps in health outcomes between Aboriginal and non-Aboriginal communities, and to publish annual progress reports and assess long-term trends.
- 20. In order to address the jurisdictional disputes concerning Aboriginal people who do not reside on reserves, we call upon the federal government to recognize, respect, and address the distinct health needs of the Métis, Inuit, and off-reserve Aboriginal peoples.

- 21. We call upon the federal government to provide sustainable funding for existing and new Aboriginal healing centers to address the physical, mental, emotional, and spiritual harms caused by residential schools, and to ensure that the funding of healing centers in Nunavut and the Northwest Territories is a priority.
- 22. We call upon those who can effect change within the Canadian health-care system to recognize the value of Aboriginal healing practices and use them in the treatment of Aboriginal patients in collaboration with Aboriginal healers and Elders where requested by Aboriginal patients.
- 23. We call upon all levels of government to: increase the number of Aboriginal professionals working in the health-care field, ensure the retention of Aboriginal health-care providers in Aboriginal communities and provide cultural competency training for all health-care professionals:

    i. Increase the number of Aboriginal professionals working in the health-care field.

    ii. Ensure the retention of Aboriginal health-care providers in Aboriginal communities.

    iii. Provide cultural competency training for all health-care professionals.
- 24. We call upon medical and nursing schools in Canada to require all students to take a course dealing with Aboriginal health issues, including the history and legacy of residential schools, the United Nations Declaration on the Rights of Indigenous Peoples, Treaties and Aboriginal rights, and Indigenous teachings and practices.
- Justice
- 25. We call upon the federal government to establish a written policy that reaffirms the independence of the RCMP to investigate crimes in which the government has its own interest as a potential or real party in civil litigation.

- 26. We call upon the federal, provincial, and territorial governments to review and amend their respective statutes of limitations to ensure that they conform with the principle that governments and other entities cannot rely on limitation defences to defend legal actions of historical abuse brought by Aboriginal people.
- 27. We call upon the Federation of Law Societies of Canada to ensure that lawyers receive appropriate cultural competency training, which includes the history and legacy of residential schools, the United Nations Declaration on the Rights of Indigenous Peoples, Treaties and Aboriginal rights, Indigenous law, and Aboriginal–Crown relations.
- 28. We call upon law schools in Canada to require all law students to take a course in Aboriginal people and the law, which includes the history and legacy of residential schools, the United Nations Declaration on the Rights of Indigenous Peoples, Treaties and Aboriginal rights, Indigenous law, and Aboriginal–Crown relations.
- 29. We call upon the parties and, in particular, the federal government, to work collaboratively with plaintiffs not included in the Indian Residential Schools Settlement Agreement to have disputed legal issues determined expeditiously on an agreed set of facts.
- 30. We call upon federal, provincial, and territorial governments to commit to eliminating the over-representation of Aboriginal people in custody over the next decade, and to issue detailed annual reports that monitor and evaluate progress in doing so.
- 31. We call upon the federal, provincial, and territorial governments to provide sufficient and stable funding to implement and evaluate community sanctions that will provide realistic alternatives to imprisonment for Aboriginal offenders and respond to the underlying causes of offending.

- 32. We call upon the federal government to amend the Criminal Code to allow trial judges, upon giving reasons, to depart from mandatory minimum sentences and restrictions on the use of conditional sentences.
- 33. We call upon the federal, provincial, and territorial governments to recognize as a high priority the need to address and prevent Fetal Alcohol Spectrum Disorder and to develop, in collaboration with Aboriginal people, FASD preventive programs that can be delivered in a culturally appropriate manner.
- 34. We call upon the governments of Canada, the provinces, and territories to undertake reforms to the criminal justice system to better address the needs of offenders with Fetal Alcohol Spectrum Disorder, including:
- i. Providing increased community resources and powers for courts to ensure that FASD is properly diagnosed, and that appropriate community supports are in place for those with FASD.
ii. Enacting statutory exemptions from mandatory minimum sentences of imprisonment for offenders affected by FASD.
iii. Providing community, correctional, and parole resources to maximize the ability of people with FASD to live in the community.
iv. Adopting appropriate evaluation mechanisms to measure the effectiveness of such programs and ensure community safety.
- 35. We call upon the federal government to eliminate barriers to the creation of additional Aboriginal healing lodges within the federal correctional system.
- 36. We call upon the federal, provincial, and territorial governments to work with Aboriginal communities to provide culturally relevant services to inmates on issues such as substance abuse, family and domestic violence, and overcoming the experience of having been sexually abused.

- 37. We call upon the federal government to provide more supports for Aboriginal programming in halfway houses and parole services.
- 38. We call upon the federal, provincial, territorial, and Aboriginal governments to commit to eliminating the over representation of Aboriginal youth in custody over the next decade.
- 39. We call upon the federal government to develop a national plan to collect and publish data on the criminal victimization of Aboriginal people, including data related to homicide and family violence victimization.
- 40. We call on all levels of government, in collaboration with Aboriginal people, to create adequately funded and accessible Aboriginal-specific victim programs and services with appropriate evaluation mechanisms.
- 41. We call upon the federal government, in consultation with Aboriginal organizations, to appoint a public inquiry into the causes of, and remedies for, the disproportionate victimization of Aboriginal women and girls. The inquiry's mandate would include:

i. An investigation into missing and murdered Aboriginal women and girls.

ii. Links to the intergenerational legacy of residential schools.

- 42. We call upon the federal, provincial, and territorial governments to commit to the recognition and implementation of Aboriginal justice systems in a manner consistent with the Treaty and Aboriginal rights of Aboriginal peoples, the Constitution Act, 1982, and the United Nations Declaration on the Rights of Indigenous Peoples, endorsed by Canada in November 2012.
- 43. We call upon federal, provincial, territorial, and municipal governments to fully adopt and implement the United Nations Declaration on the Rights of Indigenous Peoples as the framework for reconciliation.

- 44. We call upon the Government of Canada to develop a national action plan, strategies, and other concrete measures to achieve the goals of the United Nations Declaration on the Rights of Indigenous Peoples.
- Royal Proclamation and Covenant of Reconciliation
- 45. We call upon the Government of Canada, on behalf of all Canadians, to jointly develop with Aboriginal peoples a Royal Proclamation of Reconciliation to be issued by the Crown. The proclamation would build on the Royal Proclamation of 1763 and the Treaty of Niagara of 1764, and reaffirm the nation-to-nation relationship between Aboriginal peoples and the Crown. The proclamation would include, but not be limited to, the following commitments:

    i. Repudiate concepts used to justify European sovereignty over Indigenous lands and peoples such as the Doctrine of Discovery and terra nullius.

    ii. Adopt and implement the United Nations Declaration on the Rights of Indigenous Peoples as the framework for reconciliation.

    iii. Renew or establish Treaty relationships based on principles of mutual recognition, mutual respect, and shared responsibility for maintaining those relationships into the future.

    iv. Reconcile Aboriginal and Crown constitutional and legal order to ensure that Aboriginal peoples are full partners in Confederation, including the recognition and integration of Indigenous laws and legal traditions in negotiation and implementation processes involving Treaties, land claims, and other constructive agreements.

- 46. We call upon the parties to the Indian Residential Schools Settlement Agreement to develop and sign a Covenant of Reconciliation that would identify principles for working collaboratively to advance reconciliation in Canadian society, , and that would include, but not be limited to:

- i. Reaffirmation of the parties' commitments to reconciliation.

ii. Repudiation of concepts used to justify European sovereignty over Indigenous lands and peoples, such as the Doctrine of Discovery and terra nullius, and the reformation of laws, governance structures, and policies within their respective institutions that continue to rely on such concepts.

iii. Full adoption and implementation of the United Nations Declaration of the Rights of Indigenous Peoples as the framework for reconciliation.

iv. Support for the renewal or establishment of Treaty relationships based on principles of mutual recognition, mutual respect, and shared responsibility for maintaining those relationships into the future.

v. Enabling those excluded from the Settlement Agreement to sign into the Covenant of Reconciliation.

vi. Enabling other parties to sign onto the Covenant of Reconciliation.

- 47. We call upon federal, provincial, territorial, and municipal governments to repudiate concepts used to justify European sovereignty over Indigenous peoples and lands, such as the Doctrine of Discovery and terra nullius, and to reform those laws, government policies, and litigation strategies that continue to rely on such concepts.

- 48. We call upon the church parties to the Settlement Agreement, and all other faith groups and interfaith social justice groups in Canada who have not already done so, to formally adopt and comply with the principles, norms, and standards of the United Nations Declaration on the Rights of Indigenous Peoples as a framework for reconciliation. This would include, but not be limited to, the following commitments:

  - i. Ensuring that their institutions, policies, programs, and practices comply with the United Nations Declaration of the

Rights of Indigenous Peoples.

ii. Respecting Indigenous peoples' right to self-determination in spiritual matters, including the right to practice, develop, and teach their own spiritual and religious traditions, customs, and ceremonies, consistent with Article 12:1 of the United Nations Declaration of the Rights of Indigenous Peoples.

iii. Engaging in ongoing public dialogue and actions to support the United Nations Declaration of the Rights of Indigenous Peoples.

iv. Issuing a statement no later than March 31, 2016, from all religious denominations and faith groups, as to how they will implement the United Nations Declaration of the Rights of Indigenous Peoples....

- 49. We call upon all religious denominations and faith groups who have not already done so to repudiate concepts used to justify European sovereignty over Indigenous lands and peoples, such as the Doctrine of Discovery and terra nullius.
- Equity for Aboriginal People in the Legal System
- 50. In keeping with the United Nations Declaration on the Rights of Indigenous Peoples, we call upon the federal government, in collaboration with Aboriginal organizations, to fund the establishment of Indigenous law institutes for the development, use, and understanding of Indigenous laws and access to justice in accordance with the unique cultures of Aboriginal peoples in Canada.
- 51. We call upon the Government of Canada, as an obligation of its fiduciary responsibility, to develop a policy of transparency by publishing legal opinions it develops and upon which it acts or intends to act, in regard to the scope and extent of Aboriginal and Treaty rights.
- 52. We call upon the Government of Canada, provincial and territorial governments, and the courts to adopt the following legal principles:

- i. Aboriginal title claims are accepted once the Aboriginal claimant has established occupation over a particular territory at a particular point in time.
  ii. Once Aboriginal title has been established, the burden of proving any limitations on any rights arising from the existence of that title shifts to the party asserting such a limitation....
- National Council for Reconciliation
- 53. We call upon the Parliament of Canada, in consultation and collaboration with Aboriginal peoples, to enact legislation to establish a National Council for Reconciliation. The legislation would establish the council as an independent, national, oversight body with membership jointly appointed by the Government of Canada and national Aboriginal organizations, and consisting of Aboriginal and non-Aboriginal members. Its mandate would include, but not be limited to, the following:
- i. Monitor, evaluate, and report annually to Parliament and the people of Canada on the Government of Canada's post-apology progress on reconciliation to ensure that government accountability for reconciling the relationship between Aboriginal peoples and the Crown is maintained in the coming years.
  ii. Monitor, evaluate, and report to Parliament and the people of Canada on reconciliation progress across all levels and sectors of Canadian society, including the implementation of the Truth and Reconciliation Commission of Canada's Calls to Action.
  iv. Develop and implement a multi-year National Action Plan for Reconciliation, which includes research and policy development, public education programs, and resources.
  v. Promote public dialogue, public/private partnerships, and public initiatives for reconciliation.
- 54. We call upon the Government of Canada to provide multi-year funding for the National Council for Reconciliation to ensure that it has the financial, human, and technical resources required to conduct its work, including the endowment of a Na-

tional Reconciliation Trust to advance the cause of reconciliation.

- 55. We call upon all levels of government to provide annual reports or any current data requested by the National Council for Reconciliation so that it can report on the progress towards reconciliation. The reports or data would include, but not be limited to:
- i. The number of Aboriginal children – including Métis and Intuit children – in care, compared with non-Aboriginal children, the reasons for apprehension, and the total spending on preventative and care services by child-welfare agencies.

  ii. Comparative funding for the education of First Nations children on and off reserve.

  iii. The educational and income attainments of Aboriginal peoples in Canada compared with non-Aboriginal peoples.

  iv. Progress on closing the gaps between Aboriginal and non-Aboriginal communities in a number of health indicators such as: infant mortality, maternal health, suicide, mental health, addictions, life expectancy, birth rates, infant and child health issues, chronic diseases, illness and injury incidence, and the availability of appropriate health services.

  v. Progress on eliminating the overrepresentation of Aboriginal children in youth custody over the next decade.

  vi. Progress on reducing the rate of criminal victimization of Aboriginal people, including data related to homicide and family violence victimization and other crimes.

  vii. Progress on reducing the overrepresentation of Aboriginal people in the justice and correctional systems.
- 56. We call upon the prime minister of Canada to formally respond to the report of the National Council for Reconciliation by issuing an annual "State of Aboriginal Peoples" report, which would outline the government's plans for advancing the cause of reconciliation.

- Professional Development and Training for Public Servants
- 57. We call upon federal, provincial, territorial, and municipal governments to provide education to public servants on the history of Aboriginal peoples, including the history and legacy of residential schools, the United Nations Declaration on the Rights of Indigenous Peoples, Treaties and Aboriginal rights, Indigenous law, and Aboriginal–Crown relations. This will require skills-based training in intercultural competency, conflict resolution, human rights, and anti-racism.
- Church Apologies and Reconciliation
- 58. We call upon the Pope to issue an apology to survivors, their families, and communities for the Roman Catholic Church's role in the spiritual, cultural, emotional, physical, and sexual abuse of First Nations, Inuit, and Métis children in Catholic-run residential schools.
- 59. We call upon church parties to the settlement agreement to develop ongoing education strategies to ensure that their respective congregations learn about their church's role in colonization, the history and legacy of residential schools, and why apologies to former residential school students, their families, and communities were necessary.
- 60. We call upon leaders of the church parties to the settlement agreement and all other faiths, in collaboration with Indigenous spiritual leaders, survivors, schools of theology, seminaries, and other religious training centres, to develop and teach curriculum for all student clergy, and all clergy and staff who work in Aboriginal communities, on the need to respect Indigenous spirituality in its own right, the history and legacy of residential schools and the roles of the church parties in that system, the history and legacy of religious conflict in Aboriginal families and communities, and the responsibility that churches have to mitigate such conflicts and prevent spiritual violence.

- 61. We call upon church parties to the settlement agreement, in collaboration with survivors and representatives of Aboriginal organizations, to establish permanent funding to Aboriginal people for:
- i. Community-controlled healing and reconciliation projects.

ii. Community-controlled culture- and language- revitalization projects.

iii. Community-controlled education and relationship-building projects.

iv. Regional dialogues for Indigenous spiritual leaders and youth to discuss Indigenous spirituality, self-determination, and reconciliation.

- Education for Reconciliation
- 62. We call upon the federal, provincial, and territorial governments, in consultation and collaboration with survivors, Aboriginal peoples, and educators, to:
- i. Make age-appropriate curriculum on residential schools, Treaties, and Aboriginal peoples' historical and contemporary contributions to Canada a mandatory education requirement for Kindergarten to Grade Twelve students.

ii. Provide the necessary funding to post-secondary institutions to educate teachers on how to integrate Indigenous knowledge and teaching methods into classrooms.

iii. Provide the necessary funding to Aboriginal schools to utilize Indigenous knowledge and teaching methods into classrooms.

iv. Establish senior-level positions in government at the assistant deputy minister level or higher dedicated to Aboriginal content in education.

- 63. We call upon the Council of Ministers of Education, Canada to maintain an annual commitment to Aboriginal education issues, including:

- i. Developing and implementing Kindergarten to Grade Twelve curriculum and learning resources on Aboriginal peoples in Canadian history, and the history and legacy of residential schools.
  ii. Sharing information and best practices on teaching curriculum related to residential schools and Aboriginal history.
  iii. Building student capacity for intercultural understanding, empathy, and mutual respect.
  iv. Identifying teacher-training needs relating to the above.
- 64. We call upon all levels of government that provide public funds to denominational schools to require such schools to provide an education on comparative religious studies, which must include a segment on Aboriginal spiritual beliefs and practices developed in collaboration with Aboriginal elders.
- 65. We call upon the federal government, through the Social Sciences and Humanities Research Council, and in collaboration with Aboriginal peoples, post-secondary institutions and educators, and the National Centre for Truth and Reconciliation and its partner institutions, to establish a national research program with multi-year funding to advance understanding of reconciliation.
- Youth Programs
- 66. We call upon the federal government to establish multi-year funding for community-based youth organizations to deliver programs on reconciliation, and establish a national network to share information and best practices.
- Museums and Archives
- 67. We call upon the federal government to provide funding to the Canadian Museums Association to undertake, in collaboration with Aboriginal peoples, a national review of museum policies and best practices to determine the level of compliance with the United Nations Declaration on the Rights of Indigenous Peoples and to make recommendations.

- 68. We call upon the federal government, in collaboration with Aboriginal peoples, and the Canadian Museums Association to mark the 150th anniversary of Canadian Confederation in 2017 by establishing a dedicated national funding program for commemoration projects on the theme of reconciliation.
- 69. We call upon Library and Archives Canada to:
- i. Fully adopt and implement the United Nations Declaration on the Rights of Indigenous Peoples and the United Nations Joinet-Orentlicher principles, as related to Aboriginal peoples' inalienable right to know the truth about what happened and why, with regard to human rights violations committed against them in the residential schools.

ii. Ensure that its record holdings related to residential schools are accessible to the public.

iii. Commit more resources to its public education materials and programming on residential schools.

- 70) We call upon the federal government to provide funding to the Canadian Association of Archivists to undertake, in collaboration with Aboriginal peoples, a national review of archival policies and best practices to:
- i. Determine the level of compliance with the United Nations Declaration of the Rights on Indigenous Peoples and the United Nations Joinet-Orentlicher Principles, as related to Aboriginal peoples' inalienable right to know the truth about what happened and why, with regard to human rights violations committed against them in the residential schools.

ii. Produce a report with recommendations for full implementation of these international mechanisms as a reconciliation framework for Canadian archives.

- Missing Children and Burial Information
- 71. We call upon all chief coroners and provincial vital statistics agencies that have not provided to the Truth and Reconciliation Commission of Canada their records on the deaths of

Aboriginal children in the care of residential school authorities to make these documents available to the National Centre for Truth and Reconciliation.

- 72. We call upon the federal government to allocate sufficient resources to the National Centre for Truth and Reconciliation to allow it to develop and maintain the National Residential School Student Death Register established by the Truth and Reconciliation Commission of Canada.
- 73. We call upon the federal government to work with churches, Aboriginal communities, and former residential school students to establish and maintain an online registry of residential school cemeteries, including, where possible, plot maps showing the location of deceased residential school children.
- 74. We call upon the federal government to work with the churches and Aboriginal community leaders to inform the families of children who died at residential schools of the child's burial location, and to respond to families' wishes for appropriate commemoration ceremonies and markers, and reburial in home communities where requested.
- 75. We call upon the federal government to work with provincial, territorial, and municipal governments, churches, Aboriginal communities, former residential school students, and current landowners to develop and implement strategies and procedures for the ongoing identification, documentation, maintenance, commemoration, and protection of residential school cemeteries or other sites at which residential school children were buried.
- 76) We call upon the parties engaged in the work of documenting, maintaining, commemorating, and protecting residential school cemeteries to adopt strategies in accordance with the following principles:
  - i. The Aboriginal community most affected shall lead the development of such strategies.
  - ii. Information shall be sought from residential school Survivors

and other Knowledge Keepers in the development of such strategies.

iii. Aboriginal protocols shall be respected before any potentially invasive technical inspection and investigation of a ceremony site.

- National Centre for Truth and Reconciliation
- 77. We call upon provincial, territorial, municipal, and community archives to work collaboratively with the National Centre for Truth and Reconciliation to identify and collect copies of all records relevant to the history and legacy of the residential school system, and to provide these to the National Centre for Truth and Reconciliation.
- 78. We call upon the Government of Canada to commit to making a funding contribution of $10 million over seven years to the National Centre for Truth and Reconciliation, plus an additional amount to assist communities to research and produce histories of their own residential school experience and their involvement in truth, healing, and reconciliation.
- Commemoration
- 79. We call upon the federal government, in collaboration with Survivors, Aboriginal organizations, and the arts community, to develop a reconciliation framework for Canadian heritage and commemoration. This would include, but not limited to:
- i. Amending the Historic Sites and Monuments Act in include First Nations, Inuit, and Métis representation on the Historic Sites and Monuments Board of Canada and its Secretariat.

ii. Revising the policies, criteria, and practices of the National Program of Historical Commemoration to integrate Indigenous history, heritage values, and memory practices into Canada's national heritage and history.

iii. Developing and implementing a national heritage plan and strategy for commemorating residential school sites, the history

and legacy of residential schools, and the contributions of Aboriginal peoples to Canada's history.
- 80. We call upon the federal government, in collaboration with Aboriginal peoples, to establish, as a statutory holiday, a National Day for Truth and Reconciliation to honour Survivors, their families, and communities, and ensure that public commemoration of the history and legacy of residential schools remains a vital component of the reconciliation process.
- 81. We call upon the federal government, in collaboration with survivors and their organizations, and other parties to the Settlement Agreement, to commission and install a publicly accessible, highly visible, Residential Schools National Monument in the city of Ottawa to honour Survivors and all the children who were lost to their families and communities.
- 82. We call upon provincial and territorial governments, in collaboration with Survivors and their organizations, and other parties to the Settlement Agreement, to commission and install a publicly accessible, highly visible, Residential Schools Monument in each capital city to honour Survivors and all the children who were lost to their families and communities.
- 83. We call upon the Canada Council for the Arts to establish, as a funding priority, a strategy for Indigenous and non-Indigenous artists to undertake collaborative projects and produce works that contribute to the reconciliation process.
- Media and Reconciliation
- 84. We call upon the federal government to restore and increase funding to the CBC/ Radio-Canada, to enable Canada's national public broadcaster to support reconciliation, and be properly reflective of the diverse cultures, languages, and perspectives of Aboriginal peoples, including, but not limited to:
  - i. Increasing Aboriginal programming, including Aboriginal-language speakers.

  ii. Increasing equitable access for Aboriginal peoples to jobs, leadership positions, and professional development opportunities within the organization.

iii. Continuing to provide dedicated news coverage and online public information resources on issues of concern to Aboriginal peoples and all Canadians, including the history and legacy of residential schools and the reconciliation process.

- 85. We call upon the Aboriginal Peoples Television Network, as an independent non-profit broadcaster with programming by, for, and about Aboriginal peoples, to support reconciliation, including but not limited to:
- i. Continuing to provide leadership in programming and organizational culture that reflects the diverse cultures, languages, and perspectives of Aboriginal peoples.

ii. Continuing to develop media initiatives that inform and educate the Canadian public, and connect Aboriginal and non-Aboriginal Canadians.

- 86. We call upon Canadian journalism programs and media schools to require education for all students on the history of Aboriginal peoples, including the history and legacy of residential schools, the United Nations Declaration on the Rights of Indigenous Peoples, Treaties and Aboriginal rights, Indigenous law, and Aboriginal–Crown relations.
- Sports and Reconciliation
- 87. We call upon all levels of government, in collaboration with Aboriginal peoples, sports halls of fame, and other relevant organizations, to provide public education that tells the national story of Aboriginal athletes in history.
- 88. We call upon all levels of government to take action to ensure long-term Aboriginal athlete development and growth, and continued support for the North American Indigenous Games, including funding to host the games and for provincial and territorial team preparation and travel.

- 89. We call upon the federal government to amend the Physical Activity and Sport Act to support reconciliation by ensuring that policies to promote physical activity as a fundamental element of health and well-being, reduce barriers to sports participation, increase the pursuit of excellence in sport, and build capacity in the Canadian sport system, are inclusive of Aboriginal peoples.
- 90. We call upon the federal government to ensure that national sports policies, programs, and initiatives are inclusive of Aboriginal peoples, including, but not limited to:
- i. In collaboration with provincial and territorial governments, stable funding for, and access to, community sports programs that reflect the diverse cultures and traditional sporting activities of Aboriginal peoples.

  ii. An elite athlete development program for Aboriginal athletes.

  iii. Programs for coaches, trainers, and sports officials that are culturally relevant for Aboriginal peoples.

  iv. Anti-racism awareness and training programs.
- 91. We call upon the officials and host countries of international sporting events such as the Olympics, Pan Am, and Commonwealth games to ensure that Indigenous peoples' territorial protocols are respected, and local Indigenous communities are engaged in all aspects of planning and participating in such events.
- Business and Reconciliation
- 92. We call upon the corporate sector in Canada to adopt the United Nations Declaration on the Rights of Indigenous Peoples as a reconciliation framework and to apply its principles, norms, and standards to corporate policy and core operational activities involving Indigenous peoples and their lands and resources. This would include, but not limited to, the following:
- i. Commit to meaningful consultation, building respectful relationships, and obtaining the free, prior, and informed consent

of Indigenous peoples before proceeding with economic development projects.

ii. Ensure that Aboriginal peoples have equitable access to jobs, training, and educational opportunities in the corporate sector, and that Aboriginal communities gain long-term sustainable benefits from economic development projects.

iii. Provide education for management and staff on the history of Aboriginal peoples, including the history and legacy of residential schools, the United Nations Declaration on the Rights of Indigenous Peoples, Treaties and Aboriginal rights, Indigenous law, and Aboriginal-Crown relations. This will require skills based training in intercultural competency, conflict resolution, human rights, and anti-racism.

- Newcomers to Canada
- 93. We call upon the federal government, in collaboration with the national Aboriginal organizations, to revise the information kit for newcomers to Canada and its citizenship test to reflect a more inclusive history of the diverse Aboriginal peoples of Canada, including information about the Treaties and the history of residential schools.
- 94. We call upon the government of Canada to replace the oath of citizenship with the following:

"I swear (or affirm) that I will be faithful and bear true allegiance to Her Majesty Queen Elizabeth II, Queen of Canada, her heirs and successors, and that I will faithfully observe the laws of Canada including Treaties with Indigenous Peoples, and fulfill my duties as a Canadian citizen."
(TRC Canada, 2015,)

19

Empty Apologies?

Starting in 2008, due largely to the pressure of grassroots protests and organizations, the government would start to make public apologies. Leading the way would be Prime Minister Stephen Harper in 2008 for the governments historical role in the residential school system. Almost a decade later Justin Trudeau would finish off that apology. In addition to the federal apologies, Manitoba (2015), Alberta (2018), and Saskatchewan (2019), would add their apologies to the pile for their respective government's roles in the "sixties scoop." While the apologies do add a level a reality to the atrocities for future generations, they risk shutting the lid on a situation that is far from resolved and is in fact ongoing. Here are 3 of those apologies, read for yourself and decide how sincere they were.

Stephen Harper
June11, 2008
"Mr. Speaker, I stand before you today to offer an apology to former students of Indian residential schools. The treatment of children in Indian residential schools is a sad chapter in our history. In the 1870's, the federal government, partly in order to meet its obligation to educate aboriginal children, began to play a role in the development and administration of these schools.

Two primary objectives of the residential schools system were to remove and isolate children from the influence of their homes, families, traditions and cultures, and to assimilate them into the dominant culture. These objectives were based on the assumption aboriginal cultures and spiritual beliefs were inferior and unequal. Indeed, some sought, as it was infamously said, "to kill the Indian in the child."

Today, we recognize that this policy of assimilation was wrong, has caused great harm, and has no place in our country. Most schools were operated as "joint ventures" with Anglican, Catholic, Presbyterian or United churches. The government of Canada built an educational system in which very young children were often forcibly removed from their homes, often taken far from their communities. Many were inadequately fed, clothed and housed. All were deprived of the care and nurturing of their parents, grandparents and communities.

First Nations, Inuit and Métis languages and cultural practices were prohibited in these schools. Tragically, some of these children died while attending residential schools and others never returned home.

The government now recognizes that the consequences of the Indian residential schools policy were profoundly negative and that this policy has had a lasting and damaging impact on aboriginal culture, heritage and language. While some former students have spoken positively about their experiences at residential schools, these stories are far overshadowed by tragic accounts of the emotional, physical and sexual abuse and neglect of helpless children, and their separation from powerless families and communities.

The legacy of Indian residential schools has contributed to social problems that continue to exist in many communities today. It has taken extraordinary courage for the thousands of survivors that have come forward to speak publicly about the abuse they suffered. It is a testament to their resilience as individuals and to the strength of their cultures. Regrettably, many former students are not with us today and died never having received a full apology from the government of Canada. The government recognizes that the absence of an apology has been an impediment to healing and reconciliation.

Therefore, on behalf of the government of Canada and all Canadians, I stand before you, in this chamber so central to our life as a country, to apologize to aboriginal peoples for Canada's role in the Indian residential schools system.

To the approximately 80,000 living former students, and all family members and communities, the government of Canada now recognizes that it was wrong to forcibly remove children from their homes and we apologize for having done this.

We now recognize that it was wrong to separate children from rich and vibrant cultures and traditions, that it created a void in many lives and communities, and we apologize for having done this.

We now recognize that, in separating children from their families, we undermined the ability of many to adequately parent their own children and sowed the seeds for generations to follow, and we apologize for having done this.

We now recognize that, far too often, these institutions gave rise to abuse or neglect and were inadequately controlled, and we apologize for failing to protect you.

Not only did you suffer these abuses as children, but as you became parents, you were powerless to protect your own children from suffering the same experience, and for this we are sorry.

The burden of this experience has been on your shoulders for far too long. The burden is properly ours as a government, and as a country. There is no place in Canada for the attitudes that inspired the Indian residential schools system to ever again prevail. You have been working on recovering from this experience for a long time and in a very real sense, we are now joining you on this journey.

The government of Canada sincerely apologizes and asks the forgiveness of the aboriginal peoples of this country for failing them so profoundly. We are sorry.

In moving towards healing, reconciliation and resolution of the sad legacy of Indian residential schools, implementation of the Indian Residential Schools Settlement agreement began on September 19, 2007. Years of work by survivors, communities, and aboriginal organizations culminated in an agreement that gives us a new beginning and an opportunity to move forward together in partnership. A cornerstone of the settlement agreement is the Indian Residential Schools Truth and Reconciliation Commission.

This commission presents a unique opportunity to educate all Canadians on the Indian residential schools system. It will be a positive step in forging a new relationship between aboriginal peoples and other Canadians, a relationship based on the knowledge of our shared history, a respect for each other and a desire to move forward together with a renewed understanding that strong families, strong communities and vibrant cultures and traditions will contribute to a stronger Canada for all of us. (Harper, 2008)

Justin Trudeau

"Hello everyone. Thank you all for being here. Before we begin, I'd like recognize that we are in the homeland of the Inuit and Innu.

We are here today to acknowledge a historic wrong.
At the turn of the 20th century, the Moravian Mission and the International Grenfell Association, with the support of the provincial government, established schools with dormitory residences for Indigenous children in Newfoundland and Labrador.

Five residential schools were built and operated with the stated purpose of providing education. To Innu, Innuit, and NunatuKavut children, those who ran the schools promised better jobs, better opportunities, and a better life. And to their parents, they promised that their children would be cared for and provided for. They promised that their children would be safe at the Lockwood School in Cartwright, Makkovik Boarding School, the Nain Boarding School, the St. Anthony Orphanage and Boarding School, and the Yale School.

However, we know today that this colonial way of thinking led to practices that caused deep harm.
Children who came from the communities of Black Tickle, Cartwright, Goose Bay, Hopedale, Makkovik, Nain, Natuashish, Northwest River,

Postville, Rigolet and other parts of Newfoundland and Labrador were taken from their homes. Upon arrival, brothers and sisters were separated. They were forced to surrender their personal belongings, cut their hair, and comply with a strict set of rules – dictated by people who were perfect strangers. This marked the beginning of a new life for them – a life they had not chosen, enforced by strange faces. Punished for speaking their language, prohibited from practicing their culture, the children were isolated from their families, uprooted from their communities, and stripped of their identity. They were made to feel irrelevant and inferior. They were taught to be ashamed of who they were, of where they were from.

We know this because of the exceptional courage and strength of survivors, and other former students, who came forward and shared their stories. Because of them, we now know the truth about the abuse students suffered and the trauma they endured. Many were sorely neglected, and not properly fed, clothed, or housed. Others suffered physical, psychological, and sexual abuse. All were deprived of the love and care of their parents, families, and communities. These are the hard truths that are part of Canada's history. These are the hard truths we must confront as a society.

Today, I humbly stand before you to offer a long overdue apology to the former students of the Lockwood School in Cartwright, the Makkovik Boarding School, the Nain Boarding School, the St. Anthony Orphanage and Boarding School and the Yale School in Newfoundland and Labrador on behalf of the Government of Canada and all Canadians.

Pijâgingilagut
Apu ushtutatat

To all of you – we are sorry. To the students who experienced the indignity of this abuse, neglect, hardship, and discrimination by the individuals, institutions, and system entrusted with your care, we are sorry for the harm that was done to you. Sadly, not all former students are here with us today, having passed away without being able to hear this apology.

We are sorry for not apologizing sooner. For not righting this wrong before now. We honour their spirits – and cherish their memories. To the families, loved ones, and communities impacted by the tragic legacy of these schools:

Pijâgingilagut

Apu ushtutatat

To all of you – we are sorry. Children who returned from traumatic experiences in these schools turned to their families and communities for support only to find that their practices, cultures, and traditions had, in their absence, been eroded by colonialism. They returned to parents who had also been treated with a profound lack of respect, and to neighbors who had endured discrimination and racism. This is the climate in which students returned to their communities. This is the climate that was perpetuated for too long.

The consequences of colonialism have been felt far beyond the walls of these schools – consequences that persist from generation to generation and that continue to be felt today. For far too many students, profound cultural loss led to poverty, family violence, substance abuse, and community breakdown. It led to mental and physical health issues that have impeded their happiness and that of their family. Far too many continue to face adversity today as a result of time spent in residential schools and for that we are sorry.

We are sorry for the misguided belief that Indigenous children could only be properly provided for, cared for, or educated if they were separated from the influence of their families, traditions, and cultures. We are sorry for a time when Indigenous cultures were undervalued – when Indigenous languages, spiritual beliefs, and ways of life were falsely deemed to be inferior. This kind of thinking – the kind of thinking that led to the establishment of the residential school system and left deep scars for so many – has no place in our society. It was unacceptable then, and it is unacceptable now. For too long, Canada has let you carry this burden alone.

In 2008, the Government of Canada issued an official apology to the former students of Indian Residential Schools, but they failed to tell your story.

We know that the delay has caused you greater pain and suffering. The absence of an apology recognizing your experiences has been an impediment to healing and reconciliation. After years of feeling the sting of exclusion in residential schools, after decades of feeling like you were left behind, I can only imagine the devastation you must have felt in that moment of omission.

We acknowledge the hurt and pain this has caused you – and we assure you that your experiences will never be forgotten. It's about time we make things right. It's about time we accept responsibility and acknowledge our failings. Saying that we are sorry today is not enough. It will not erase the loneliness you have felt; it will not undo the harm you have suffered. It will not bring back the languages and traditions you have lost. It will not take away the isolation and vulnerability you felt when separated from your families, communities and cultures. It will not repair the hardships you endured in the years that followed as you struggled to recover from what you experienced in the schools and move forward with your lives.

But today I'm here to tell you, on behalf of the Government of Canada and of all Canadians, that this burden is one you no longer have to carry alone. It is my sincere hope that you can finally get some closure – that you can put your inner child to rest. That you can finally begin to heal. The treatment of Indigenous children in residential schools is a painful chapter of Canada's history that we must confront. For too long, it's a chapter we chose to skip; a chapter we chose to leave out of our textbooks. Out of shame, out of denial, Canadians and their governments have turned a blind eye on this story because it runs counter to the promise of this country and the ambition of its people. It's time for Canada to acknowledge its history for what it is: flawed, imperfect, and unfinished.

It's time for us to recognize our failings in tandem with our successes, and live up to our principles we cherish and ideals we hold. And while the history of these residential schools can never be forgotten, we cannot let it define our future. All Canadians possess the ability to learn from the past and shape the future. All Canadians have the power to be better and to do better. That is the path to reconciliation. We have an opportunity to rebuild our relationship, based on the recognition of your rights, respect, cooperation, partnership, and trust. Reconciliation between the Government of Canada and Indigenous peoples – and between Indigenous and non-Indigenous peoples – is an ongoing process.

We know that it won't happen overnight. But it is my hope that in apologizing today – in acknowledging the past and asking for forgiveness – that as a country, we will continue to advance on the path of reconciliation together. The Newfoundland and Labrador residential schools settlement is an example of reconciliation in action, a settlement with healing and commemoration at its core. All Canadians have much to learn not only from the hardship former students have endured, but from the incredible strength they have displayed in the face of adversity. The bravery shown by former students, who made this settlement possible, and the resilience displayed by entire communities cannot be overstated. I hope that you will continue to tell your stories – in your own way and in your own words – as this healing and commemoration process unfolds. Let this day mark the beginning of a new chapter in our history – one in which we vow to never forget the harm we have caused you and vow to renew our relationship.

Let this new chapter be one in which Indigenous and non-Indigenous people build the future they want together.

Tshinashkumitin,
Nakummek.
Thank you."
(Trudeau, 2017)

Premier Rachel Notley

May 28, 2018

"I'd like to begin by acknowledging that we are gathered here today on the traditional territory of Treaty 6, and I'd also like to acknowledge the Métis people of Alberta who share a very deep connection with this land. I rise today in the spirit of truth and reconciliation. Before we begin, I'd like us all to take a moment and just look up.

When we speak about colonialism and its vestiges, when we speak about the need for truth and reconciliation here in Alberta and across Canada, when we speak about healing, we must remember always that we speak about people. Above us today are survivors of the Sixties Scoop: women and men, children and grandchildren, parents and grandparents, all of them survivors.

As we speak today in their presence, we are mindful that their presence carries with it also a terrible absence; parents lost; children taken; families destroyed; cultures shamed, ignored, and forgotten; by force, a proud way of life taken away. The decisions that led to that personal trauma: many of those decisions, Mr. Speaker, were made right here on this floor in this Chamber.

The Government of Alberta owes these people an apology, and today that's what we are here to do. But for that apology to have the meaning that these women and men deserve, these women and men deserve to know that their experiences were heard and are heard and are understood as best we can. These women and men deserve to know that we stand here today looking up at them not only with hearts of reconciliation but with eyes that see the wrongs of the past as clearly as we can.

So before we can offer our apology, please allow me to speak to the work done to make this apology meaningful for these brave women and men, because they deserve nothing less.

The Sixties Scoop is the colloquial name for the government practices perpetuated in Alberta and across Canada from the 1950s to the 1980s. Indigenous children were taken from their birth families, from their communities, put in non-Indigenous homes, without meaningful steps, in some cases without any steps at all, to preserve their culture, their identity, their relationship with their community, and, even most importantly, with their family.

To speak of the Sixties Scoop in these terms is to speak merely of the broadest and the most impersonal strokes. To appreciate the trauma these women and men lived through, we need to hear it from them in their voices, and that's what we set out to do. Over 800 courageous survivors of the Sixties Scoop shared with us their heartbreaking experiences, and I want to thank each and every person who participated in that.

All of you who came forward and shared your experiences did so with courage beyond measure. You didn't just share the trauma of what was done to you; you spoke truth to power. You spoke truth to the same power, the same institution, and the government that inflicted this trauma on you in the first place. So to all of you, thank you.

The stories that you, the survivors, shared with us are heartbreaking. These stories transcend generations: children – kids, babies, toddlers, teens – ripped from your families; parents unable to see through the tears as they took your children away from you; grandparents forced aside as your families were destroyed.

We heard stories of how you were lied to and told that your families didn't want you or couldn't care for you. We heard how many of you were never told where your children had gone, where your parents had gone, where your brothers or sisters had gone.

Many of you were placed into foster care, with no linkages to your culture, bounced from home to home, place to place, with no stability or sense of who you are and the proud place that you came from. We also heard clearly that some of those foster homes were also not safe. Many of you faced terrible abuse – physical abuse, sexual abuse, mental and emotional abuse – forced labour, starvation, and neglect. A survivor shared this quote with us, and I want to share it today because I believe it reveals the horror and the tragedy of what was done to these children. That person said:

"I was abused in every home. The worst part was that we actually had a family that loved us."

Many of you shared that even as children you contemplated suicide. Those feelings were often compounded by the isolation that you experienced.

When you were placed in non-Indigenous homes and communities, the dominance of colonial thinking meant that you regularly faced racism and discrimination. Some of you were forbidden to speak your own language, forced instead to speak English or French. Many of you were not allowed to honour or express your culture. Make no mistake. The Sixties Scoop was an assault on Indigenous identity, your sense of self and who you are.

As a result, many of you never felt at home anywhere, not in the homes and communities where you were fostered or adopted and not even when you returned home. One survivor remembered:

"At 19 I went back to the reserve. One minute I am white. One minute I am red. I never knew which side I belonged on."

Another said:

"I lost my spirit. It was taken away from me."

The impacts of these government actions are still felt by you and your families today. The scars of this tragedy still linger, some as fresh as they were a generation ago. Many of you told us that you still experience family dysfunction and difficult relationships as a result of what was done to you. Some survivors shared that they never felt love during childhood. One survivor said, "I couldn't understand what real love was."

Many of you struggle with self-identity due to losing your culture, your language, and the connection to your families. Many of you spoke about ongoing challenges with government systems and education and police and justice. When we look clearly at what was done to you, what we did to you, it is no wonder that it is so hard for so many of you to trust again.

Many survivors spoke about poor physical and mental health, about drug and alcohol addiction, about depression and suicide and early deaths amongst families and friends. The legacy of residential schools was and is a constant shadow over your lives. Many of you had parents and grandparents who were traumatized by residential schools. These traumas were often passed on to you, and many survivors spoke of the ongoing trauma their parents experienced.

Many fear that they passed this trauma on to their children. A survivor told us, "The cycle needs to stop," and we agree. I ask again for the members of this Assembly to look up, to see these survivors, to honour them and their ancestors with our full attention.

To you, the survivors of the Sixties Scoop, to your children, to your parents, to the rest of your families, and to your communities, from me as Premier of Alberta, from all of us here as the elected representatives of the people of Alberta, and on behalf of the government of Alberta, we are sorry.

For the loss of families, of stability, of love, we are sorry.

For the loss of identity, of language and culture, we are sorry.

For the loneliness, the anger, the confusion, and the frustration, we are sorry.

For the government practice that left you Indigenous people estranged from your families and your communities and your history, we are sorry.

For this trauma, this pain, this suffering, alienation, and sadness, we are sorry.

To all of you, I am sorry.

In Cree the word is ni mihtâtam.

In Dene the word is bek'e nasdlí.

In Beaver the word is sekaa-tah.

In Nakota the word is wécã ptac.

In Blackfoot the closest term is tsik skâp(h) tsap spinaa'n.

In Soto the closest term is gaween-ouchi-dahh-do-taw-naan.

In Michif the term is ni mihtatayn.

We are sorry.

For an apology to be worth anything, it must also carry with it a promise.

Here is my promise, our promise, to the survivors of the Sixties Scoop.

We will work with Indigenous communities, with each of you. We will ensure that your perspectives, your desires, and your priorities for your families and communities are reflected in what we do going forward. No one knows what Indigenous children and families need better than First Nation, Métis, and Inuit communities. We will honour that.

We will work together with you, your families, your elders, and your communities to correct historical injustices and find a path to true reconciliation between our government and Indigenous Albertans.

Together we can help heal the wounds of the past, together we can ensure that Indigenous children grow up happy and healthy and connected to their families, their communities, and their cultures, and together we will ensure that all Indigenous Albertans enjoy the same privileges and opportunities as every Albertan. With all of this work we are not starting from a standstill.

The work that began with the Sixties Scoop consultation continues, and the relationship being built through those consultations, a relationship that we hope is a new and growing form of trust, will serve us well as we continue together down the path of reconciliation.

Honoured guests, Mr. Speaker, members of the Assembly, thank you for the privilege of speaking with you today and for the opportunity to express our deepest apologies for the government practice known as the Sixties Scoop.

Before I conclude, I do want to acknowledge the amazing work of the Sixties Scoop Indigenous Society of Alberta and thank them for their guidance and their leadership over the past months.

To everyone who participated in the engagement sessions over the past months and told their story, thank you again for your bravery and for putting your trust in us. We will honour that trust. Now, Mr. Speaker, I would ask that all members of the Assembly rise and join me in offering their thanks and their honour to the survivors who are with us today." (Notley, 2018)

20

Conclusion

Thirteen years later and those heartfelt words appear to be just that, words. Despite all the apologies, commissions, and good intentions, little appears to change. While our current Prime Minister, Justin Trudeau is always keen to say the right thing or snap the right selfie, actual change and work toward real reconciliation continues to be hindered, largely, by the Canadian government. It continues to say the right thing, while continuing to block legislation, abstain from progressive Indigenous rights votes, and support infrastructure through Indigenous lands with or without band approval. Coming to power in 2015 Prime Minister Justin Trudeau promised to end all long-term boil water advisories on Reserves by March 2021. As of July 2021, this date has been pushed back until 2024-2026, despite providing 6.1 billion dollars in foreign aid in 2018 and 6.1 billion in 2019. I'm sure 12 billion dollars would solve an awful lot of drinking water problems.

Last week (July 7th, 2021) Prime Minister Trudeau visited the Cowessess First Nation, a community recently rocked by the discovery of 751 unmarked graves, mostly children. Trudeau was sure to visit the site and snap a few pictures of him leaving teddy bears at unmarked graves. Meanwhile, last month, Trudeau and his cabinet abstained from a vote to quit fighting Indigenous communities over child welfare battles in court, a motion that received a 279-0 with support from all parties, including several liberal MP's, Justin's entire cabinet did not cast a vote. We will end this book on an upswing. Last week, Friday, July 9th 2021, the Cowessess First Nation became the first Indigenous Nation in

Canada to take back control of its child welfare, a system that had been in the hands of the federal or provincial governments for over 70 years. In a province where 86% of the children in care are First Nations and they continue to battle the ongoing trauma from generations abuse, this is no small achievement. The federal government has pledged just over 38 million to help with implementation.

With a little luck we can hope that this is the new trend, the dawn of a new day for Canada and the Indigenous People. For the first time in a century and a half, through education, the Canadian and Indigenous people themselves can work towards a brighter future together, and our children can grow up together in a world that celebrates our differences as opposed to registering, filing, and dividing us with them.

In closing, I'm reminded of last year's statement from the Hopi Indian Chief White Eagle, whose statement in March of 2020 reminded us all that in every moment the choice for the future is individually ours, with collective implications. Canada has come to a crossroads in its history, we can either open the door, or fall into the hole. We can either fall back into our holes of ignorance, or we can open the door, have real conversations, and start the path to true reconciliation.

Miigwech
(Thank You)
   The End

21

Bibliography

Bibliography

1) Mathisen, D.W. (2014). The Undying Stars: The truth that unites the world's ancient wisdom and the conspiracy to keep it from you. Beowulf Books.
2) Erdoes, R. & Ortiz, A. (1984). American Indian: Myths and Legends. Pantheon Books.
3) Harris, K. (June 17, 2020). Canada loses its bid for seat on UN Security Council. (Article). Re-trieved from https://www.cbc.ca/news/politics/united-nations-security-council-canada-1.5615488)
4) CBC News. (Sep 13, 2007). Canada votes 'no' as UN native rights declaration passes. (Article). Retrieved from https://www.cbc.ca/news/canada/canada-votes-no-as-un-native-rights-declaration-passes-1.632160
5) Indian Act of 1985, R.S.C. c. I-5. (2019). Re-trieved from https://laws-lois.justice.gc.ca/eng/acts/I-5/FullText.html
6) Biggar, E.B. (1891). Anecdotal life of Sir John A Macdonald. John Lovell & Son.
7) Canada, House of Commons Debates (9 May 1883). (PDF). Re-trieved from https://www.canadiana.ca/view/oocihm.9_07186_1_2/2?r=0&s=1

8) Canada, House of Commons Debates. (17 May 1882). (PDF). Retrieved from https://play.google.com/store/books/details?id=oYRYAAAAYAAJ&rdid=book-oYRYAAAAYAAJ&rdot=1

9) Scott, D.C. (1926) The Poems of Duncan Camp-bell Scott. McClelland and Stewart.

10) Titley, B. (1986). A Narrow Vision: Duncan Campbell Scott and the Administration of Indi-an. University of British Columbia Press.

11) National Archives of Canada, Record Group 10, volume 6810, file 470-2-3, volume 7, pp. 55 (L-3) and 63 (N-3).

12) Truth and Reconciliation Commission of Cana-da. (2015). Canada's Residential Schools: The History, Part 1, Origins to 1939: The Final Re-port of the Truth and Reconciliation Commission of Canada, Volume I. (PDF). McGill-Queen's Uni-versity Press. Retrieved from http://www.trc.ca/assets/pdf/Volume_1_History_Part_1_English_Web.pdf

13) Bryce P. (1922). The story of a national crime: being a record of the health conditions of the Indians of Canada from 1904 to 1921. Ottawa: James Hope and Sons. 3.

14) Bryce PH. (1907). Report on the Indian schools of Manitoba and the North-West Territo-ries. Ottawa: Government Printing Bureau.

15) The Indian Act said what? (PDF). Retrieved from https://www.nwac.ca/wp-content/uploads/2018/04/The-Indian-Act-Said-WHAT-pdf-1.pdf

16) Edmond, J. (July 7, 2014). Indian Residential Schools: A Chronology (Blog). Retrieved from https://www.lawnow.org/indian-residential-schools-chronology/

17) Annett, K. (2016). Murder by Decree: The Crime of Genocide in Canada (PDF). The Inter-national Tribunal for the Disappeared of Canada (ITDC). Retrieved from https://.murderbydecree.com

18) The Truth Commission into Genocide in Cana-da. (2007) Hidden from History: The Canadian Holocaust (PDF). Retrieved from http://canadiangenocide.nativeweb.org/genocide.pdf

19) Short, A. (2021 June 7). 'This atrocity hap-pened:' Residential schools radar work gets na-tional strategy, released funding (Arti-cle).Retrieved from https://thestarphoenix.com/news/saskatchewan/this-atrocity-happened-residential-schools-radar-work-gets-national-strategy-financial-bolster

20) Prime Minister of Canada, Justin Trudeau. (2021 June 24). State-ment by the Prime Minis-ter on the findings around the former Marieval (Cowessess) Residential School in Saskatchewan. Retrieved from https://pm.gc.ca/en/news/statements/2021/06/24/statement-prime-minister-findings-around-former-marieval-cowessess

21) Tk'emlúps te Secwépemc (Kamloops Indian Band). (2021 May 21). Office of the Chief. For immediate release. [Press release]. https://tkemlups.ca/wp-content/uploads/05-May-27-2021-TteS-MEDIA-RELEASE.pdf

22) Provincial Archives of Saskatchewan FILM R-445.5. (Video) Re-trieved from https://www.cbc.ca/player/play/1190542915827/

23) Perkel, C. (2017 October 5).'60s Scoop settle-ment 'first step' in reconciliation with Indige-nous victims: Bennett. (Article)Retrieved from https://globalnews.ca/news/3787984/federal-government-to-an-nounce-payout-of-800m-to-indigenous-victims-of-60s-scoop/

24) Sixties Scoop Class Action. (nd). Claim Sta-tistics table. Re-trieved from https://sixtiesscoopsettlement.info/

25) Johnson, R. (2018 June 26). Sixties Scoop set-tlement may be in jeopardy after Ontario judge rejects legal fees as 'excessive'. (Article). Re-trieved from https://www.cbc.ca/news/indigenous/sixties-scoop-on-tario-judge-legal-fees-excessive-1.4723469#:~:text=The%20four%20firms%20named%20in,and%20the%20Merchant%20Law%20Group.

26) The Canadian Press. (2018). Lawyer fees ap-proved in '60s Scoop class action; deal struck to allow payouts. (Article). https://www.to-dayville.com/calgary/deal-reached-over-60s-scoop-legal-costs-lawyer-personally-off-the-hook/

27) Sinclair, Raven. (2016). The Indigenous Child Removal System in Canada: An examination of legal decision-making and racial bias.

(Article). Retrieved from https://www.researchgate.net/publication/ 317054752_The_Indigenous_Child_Removal_System_in_Canada_An_examination_of_legal_decision-making_and_racial_bias

28) Indigenous Services Canada. (2018 November 30)). Federal legislation as an important step to-ward reducing the number of Indigenous children in foster care. Retrieved from https://www.canada.ca/en/indigenous-services-canada/news/2018/11/federal-legislation-as-an-important-step-toward-reducing-the-number-of-indigenous-children-in-foster-care.html

29) Statistics Canada. (2018). National Household Survey: Aboriginal Peoples Suicide among First Nations people, Métis and Inuit (2011-2016): Findings from the 2011 Canadian Census Health and Environment Cohort (CanCHEC). Retrieved from https://www150.statcan.gc.ca/n1/pub/99-011-x/99-011-x2019001-eng.htm

30) Department of Justice Canada. (2017). Missing and Murdered Indigenous Women and Girls. (PDF) Retrieved from https://www.justice.gc.ca/eng/rp-pr/jr/jf-pf/2017/docs/july04.pdf

31) Native Womens Wilderness.(nd). Murdered and Missing Indigenous Women. Retrieved from https://www.nativewomenswilderness.org/mmiw

32) Brass, M. (July 02, 2004). Starlight Tours (Ar-ticle). Retrieved from https://www.cbc.ca/news2/background/aboriginals/starlight-tours.html

33) Radford, E. (January 14, 2015). Starlight tours - a timeline. A detailed look at the events sur-rounding the death of Neil Stonechild and the subsequent inquiry. (Article) The Star Phoenix. Retrieved from (https://thestarphoenix.com/news/saskatoon/starlight-tours-a-timeline)

34) Royal Commission on Aboriginal Peoples: Al-fred Scow. (1992 November 26). Transcriptions of Public Hearings and Round Table Discussions, 1992-1993: page 344-345. Retrieved from http://digital.scaa.sk.ca/ourlegacy/permalink/30466

35)   Barron, F.L. (1988). The Indian Pass System in the Canadian West, 1882-1935. (PDF). Prairie Forum, Vol. 13, No.1. Retrieved from https://saskarchives.com/sites/default/files/barron_indianpasssystem_prairieforum_vol13_no1_pp25ff.pdf
36)   Elections Canada. (2021). A Brief History of Federal Voting Rights in Canada. Retrieved from https://electionsanddemocracy.ca/voting-rights-through-time-0/brief-history-federal-voting-rights-canada
37)   McCue, H.A. (31 May 2011). Reserves (Article. Retrieved from https://www.thecanadianencyclopedia.ca/en/article/aboriginal-reserves
38)   Government of Canada. (1969). Statement of the Government of Canada on Indian Policy, 1969.
39)   Cardinal, H. (1999). The Unjust Society. 2nd ed. Vancouver: Douglas & MacIntyre.
40)   Legace, N & Sinclair, N.J. (2015 September 24). The White Paper, 1969 (Article). The Ca-nadian Encyclopedia. Retrieved from https://www.thecanadianencyclopedia.ca/en/article/the-white-paper-1969
41)   (PDF). Retrieved from https://oneca.com/1969_White_Paper.pdf
42)   Indian Chiefs of Alberta. (1970). Citizens Plus.(PDF) Retrieved from http://caid.ca/RedPaper1970.pdf
43)   The Truth and Reconciliation Commission of Canada. (2021). Mandate Retrieved from http://www.trc.ca/about-us/our-mandate.html
44)   Truth and Reconciliation Commission of Cana-da. (2015). Calls to Action. (PDF). Retrieved from http://trc.ca/assets/pdf/Calls_to_Action_English2.pdf
45)   Harper, S. (2008 June 11). Statement of Apol-ogy – to former students of Indian Residential Schools. (PDF). Retrieved from https://www.rcaanc-cirnac.gc.ca/DAM/DAM-CIRNAC-RCAANC/DAM-RECN/STAGING/texte-text/

rqpi_apo_pdf_1322167347706_eng.pdf

46) Prime Minister of Canada, Justin Trudeau. (2017 November 24) Remarks by Prime Minis-ter Justin Trudeau to apologize on behalf of the Government of Canada to former students of the Newfoundland and Labrador residential schools. Retrieved from https://pm.gc.ca/en/news/speeches/2017/11/24/remarks-prime-minister-justin-trudeau-apologize-behalf-government-canada

47) Legislative Assembly of Alberta, Notley R. (2018 May 28). Sixties Scoop apology speech. Retrieved from https://www.alberta.ca/release.cfm?xID=560616704B9A0-C113-B187-A4BACC8308538863

48) Djuric, M. (2021 July 9). How Cowessess First Nation's historic child welfare agreement with Canada and Saskatchewan works. (Article). Re-trieved from https://www.cbc.ca/news/canada/saskatchewan/how-cowessess-first-nation-child-welfare-agreement-works-1.6095470

www.ingramcontent.com/pod-product-compliance
Lightning Source LLC
Chambersburg PA
CBHW070428010526
44118CB00014B/1944